18th Conference of the European Chapter of the Association for Computational Linguistics (EACL 2024)

Tutorial Abstracts

St. Julian's, Malta
21 - 22 March 2024

ISBN: 978-1-7138-9446-9

Printed from e-media with permission by:

Curran Associates, Inc.
57 Morehouse Lane
Red Hook, NY 12571

Some format issues inherent in the e-media version may also appear in this print version.

Association for Computational Linguistics
209 N. Eighth Street
Stroudsburg, Pennsylvania 18360

Phone: 1-570-476-8006
Fax: 1-570-476-0860

acl@aclweb.org

Additional copies of this publication are available from:

Curran Associates, Inc.
57 Morehouse Lane
Red Hook, NY 12571 USA
Phone: 845-758-0400
Fax: 845-758-2633
Email: curran@proceedings.com
Web: www.proceedings.com

EACL 2024

The 18th Conference of the European Chapter of the Association for Computational Linguistics

Proceedings of Tutorial Abstracts

March 21, 2024

The EACL organizers gratefully acknowledge the support from the following sponsors.

Platinum

Megagon Labs

Gold

Bloomberg Engineering

snowflake

Bronze

Adobe

Babelscape

D&I Champion

HITS Heidelberger Institut für Theoretische Studien

Order copies of this and other ACL proceedings from:

Association for Computational Linguistics (ACL)
317 Sidney Baker St. S
Suite 400 - 134
Kerrville, TX 78028
USA
Tel: +1-855-225-1962
acl@aclweb.org

Introduction

Welcome to the Tutorials Session of EACL 2024.

NLP is a rapidly-changing field, which has undergone different periods, and the knowledge needed to be at pace is changing rapidly. A lot of changes have been brought up by recent advances in the development and deployment of Large Language Models (LLMs). Five tutorials have been selected for this year's EACL, which reflect this trend.

The EACL tutorial session is organized to give conference attendees an introduction by expert researchers to some topics of importance drawn from our rapidly growing and changing research field.

This year, as has been the tradition over the past few years, the call, submission, reviewing, and selection of tutorials were coordinated jointly for multiple conferences: EACL, NAACL-HLT, ACL, and EMNLP.

We would like to thank the tutorial authors for their contributions and flexibility on topics including interpretability, multilingualism and multimodality.

EACL 2024 Tutorial Co-chairs
Mohsen Mesgar
Sharid Loáiciga

Organizing Committee

General Chair

Michael Strube, Heidelberg Institute for Theoretical Studies

Program Chairs

Yvette Graham, Trinity College, Dublin
Matthew Purver, Queen Mary University of London and Jožef Stefan Institute

Tutorial Chairs

Mohsen Mesgar, Bosch Center for Artificial Intelligence
Sharid Loáiciga, University of Gothenburg

Table of Contents

Computational modeling of semantic change

Pierluigi Cassotti, **Francesco Periti**, **Stefano de Pascale**,
Haim Dubossarsky, **and Nina Tahmasebi**
University of Gothenburg, University of Milan, KU Leuven/VUB
Queen Mary University of London
{nina.tahmasebi,pierluigi.cassotti}@gu.se
francesco.periti@unimi.it, stefano.depascale@kuleuven.be
h.dubossarsky@qmul.ac.uk

1 Introduction

Languages change constantly over time, influenced by social, technological, cultural and political factors that affect how people express themselves. In particular, words can undergo the process of semantic change, which can be subtle yet significantly impact the interpretation of texts. For example, the word *terrific* used to mean "causing terror" and was as such synonymous to *terrifying*. Nowadays, speakers use the word in the sense of "excessive" and even "amazing".

In Historical Linguistics, tools and methods have been developed to analyse this phenomenon, including systematic categorisations of the types of change, the causes and the mechanisms underlying the different types of change. However, traditional linguistic methods, while informative, are often based on small, carefully curated samples. Thanks to the availability of both large diachronic corpora, the tools to model word meaning using unsupervised computational methods, and evaluation benchmarks, we are seeing an increasing interest in the computational modelling of semantic change. This is evidenced by the increasing number of publications in this new domain as well as the organisation of initiatives and events related to this topic, such as the yearly workshop on Computational Approaches to Historical Language Change *LChange*[1] that reached its fourth year , and several evaluation campaigns (Schlechtweg et al., 2020a; Basile et al., 2020b; Kutuzov et al.; Zamora-Reina et al., 2022).

Relevance Computational modelling of semantic change is highly relevant for fields like lexicography but also studies in (Historical) Linguistics where we can complement and verify existing research on larger corpora, more genres, more extended periods and many more languages. Computational modelling of semantic change is also interesting for any text-based humanities and social sciences as well as technical and medical science, where the evolution of concepts or the progression of before and after is studied. In the past few years, we have seen an increasing interest in utilizing methods for semantic change in other domains. Marjanen et al. (2019) delved into the connections between "isms" (like liberalism, socialism, and conservatism) and ideological language, shedding light on the progression of political language throughout history. Bizzoni et al. (2020) investigate changes in scientific writing, while Haider and Eger (2019) direct their focus in poetry studies. Wevers (2019) and Garg et al. (2018) investigated the presence and evolution of gender biases and ethnic stereotypes in various textual data. Vylomova et al. (2019) honed in on the semantic transformations of harm-related concepts within psychology. Their study sought to determine if concepts like *addiction*, *bullying*, *harassment*, *prejudice*, and *trauma* have broadened in scope over the past forty years. Tripodi et al. (2019) traced the evolution and prevalence of antisemitic biases across various domains, such as religion, economics, and socio-politics. Their data suggested an alarming rise in antisemitism, particularly in France, from the mid-80s onward.

This tutorial will be interest of for the ACL community as a venue for facilitating discussions and sharing knowledge on Diachronic Linguistics and time-aware language analysis. There is an extensive collection of models, methods and trained diachronic resources that benefit anyone interested in temporally evolving information beyond the LSC community. Moreover, it will provide a practical demonstration of available tools to researchers and practitioners working on different aspects of LSC and historical linguistics. In particular, we

[1] https://www.changeiskey.org/event/2023-emnlp-lchange/

Proceedings of the 18th Conference of the European Chapter of the Association for Computational Linguistics
Tutorial Abstracts, pages 1–8
March 21, 2024

will showcase the benchmark developed within the Change is Key! program, in which a suit of pre-trained models, as well as training and test data, are available[2], and *integrate hands-on sessions throughout the tutorial.*

2 Tutorial overview

This tutorial will overview the current approaches, problems, and challenges in detecting lexical semantic changes. At its core, the computational modelling of semantic change consists of the following:

- Modelling of word meaning, typically using unsupervised methods applied to diachronic corpora;
- modelling of meaning change, based on the outcome of the above; and
- evaluation.

This tutorial will extend the above with an introduction to lexical semantic change and an overview of the available resources (corpora, pre-trained diachronic models, and data sets). We will highlight issues in the creation and use of diachronic corpora and different procedures for annotating data. Next, we will introduce the current state-of-the-art approaches for automatic detection of LSC, provide a hands-on section on available systems and tools, and open the floor to discuss possible applications.

3 Outline

1. Introduction to Semantic Change and Computational modeling (1.5 hours)

2. Evaluation: Tasks, benchmarks, and measurements of Lexical Semantic Change (1.5 hours)

3. Models for Lexical Semantic Change Detection (2 hours)

4. Hands-on and Discussion (1 hours)

3.1 Introduction to Semantic Change and Computational modelling (1.5 hour)

We will provide a theoretical background of LSC, paying attention to semasiological phenomena, i.e., semantic change. We will introduce the classical types of semasiological change (e.g., metaphorization/metonymization or generalization/specialization) but also focus on types of changes at the level of synonymous groups or entire lexical fields (Geeraerts, 2020). Several theories, among which diachronic prototype semantics (Geeraerts, 1997) and grammaticalization theory (Traugott, 2017), will be reviewed. Finally, we will discuss some of the theoretically relevant findings recently studied in computational semantic change (e.g., the Law of Parallel Change and the Law of Differentiation (Hamilton et al., 2016a; Liétard et al., 2023; Stern, 1921)).

3.2 Evaluation: Tasks, benchmarks, and measurements of Lexical Semantic Change (1.5 hour)

We will briefly overview some of the available most used diachronic corpora such as The New York Times corpus (Sandhaus, 2008), l'Unità corpus (Basile et al., 2020a), the DTA corpus (Textarchiv), the BZ and ND corpora (Zeitung), the CCOHA corpus (Alatrash et al.), the LatinISE corpus (McGillivray and Kilgarriff, 2013), and the KubHist corpus (Adesam et al., 2019). A list of lexicographic resources useful for Lexical Semantic Change will be described, such as the Oxford English Dictionary[3] and the Sabatini Coletti dictionary[4] (Basile et al.).

We will introduce the framework DUREL (Schlechtweg et al., 2018) for the annotation of LSC, which is employed in the annotation process of Semeval 2020 Task 1 (Schlechtweg et al., 2020a). We will present the tasks on which LSC is usually framed: Unsupervised Lexical Semantic Change Detection, Lexical Semantic Change Discovery and Temporal Analogies. For each task, we will introduce the most used benchmarks, namely SemEval-2020 Task 1: Unsupervised Lexical Semantic Change Detection (Schlechtweg et al., 2020b), which is the first task on Unsupervised Lexical Semantic Change Detection in English, German, Swedish, and Latin languages, RuShiftEval (Kutuzov and Pivovarova, 2021) for the Russian language, LSCDiscovery (Zamora-Reina et al., 2022), the Shared Task on Semantic Change Discovery and Detection in Spanish, NorDiaChange (Kutuzov et al., 2022), ChiWUG (Chen et al., 2023), and the datasets for the Temporal Analogies task (Yao et al., 2018; Szymanski, 2017).

[2] https://github.com/ChangeIsKey/LSCDBenchmark

[3] https://www.oed.com/

[4] https://dizionari.corriere.it/dizionario_italiano/

3.3 Models for Lexical Semantic Change Detection (2 hours)

We will provide some background on Distributional Semantics introducing PPMI matrices (Levy and Goldberg), Word2vec (Mikolov et al., 2013) and BERT models (Devlin et al., 2018). Then, we will present models for Lexical Semantic Change, starting from Alignment Models (Tahmasebi et al., 2021; Kutuzov et al., 2018; Cassotti et al., 2020). In particular, we will introduce Post-alignment models such as those based on Orthogonal Procrustes (Hamilton et al., 2016b), Jointly Explicit Alignment Models such as Dynamic word embeddings (Yao et al., 2018), and Jointly Implicit Alignment Models such as Temporal Word Embedding with a Compass (Carlo et al., 2019), Temporal Referencing (Dubossarsky et al., 2019) and Temporal Random Indexing (Basile et al., 2016).

With the increasing use of contextualised word embeddings, numerous approaches employing BERT-base models have been developed for LSC Detection (Montanelli and Periti, 2023; Laicher et al., 2021). We will present the approaches based on contextualised word embeddings following the classification framework proposed by Montanelli and Periti (2023). In particular, we will discuss the use of contextualised embeddings according to three dimensions of analysis: meaning representation, time-awareness, and learning modality. We will illustrate existing approaches as concrete examples for each dimension, allowing for a more precise and comprehensive understanding. For example, we will introduce simple unsupervised approaches such as the use of similarity measure like Average Pairwise Distance (Giulianelli et al., 2020), or clustering algorithms like WiDiD (Periti et al., 2022), but also supervised approaches that leverage the time information of the corpora such as TempoBERT (Rosin et al., 2022) and Temporal Attention (Rosin and Radinsky, 2022)).

Moreover, we will present approaches that train BERT models on Word Sense Disambiguation (Navigli, 2009) and Word-in-Context (Pilehvar and Camacho-Collados, 2019) tasks to perform LSC Detection such as GlossReader (Rachinskiy and Arefyev, 2021), DeepMistake (Arefyev et al., 2021), and XL-LEXEME (Cassotti et al., 2023). Finally, we will look at models based on lexical substitution, such as Card (2023) and Liétard et al. (2023), and generative models (Giulianelli et al., 2023).

4 Tutorial Information

Type of the tutorial Introductory.

Length This is a 6-hour tutorial.

Target audience and background This tutorial targets researchers at different levels of expertise in the field. Introductory researchers will gain a comprehensive understanding of the topic, covering foundational concepts and available resources. Intermediate researchers will deepen their knowledge with advanced approaches for automatic detection and analysis of LSC, while advanced researchers will explore state-of-the-art techniques and address complex challenges. The tutorial is designed to be inclusive, fostering the participation of attendees with varying experience levels. Furthermore, the tutorial aims to foster a more powerful synergy between the LSC domain and other areas of NLP, particularly emphasising the integration with Lexical Semantics and research pursuits in Word Sense Discrimination. Prerequisites include a basic understanding of linguistics, Natural Language Processing, and Computational Linguistics concepts.

Breadth The tutorial sections will cover both works from the tutorial presenters and others:

- Introduction to Language Change: 20% of work by tutorial presenters and 80% by others
- Evaluation: Tasks, benchmarks, and measurements of Lexical Semantic Change: 40% of work by tutorial presenters and 60% by others
- Models for Lexical Semantic Change Detection: 20% of work by tutorial presenters and 80% by others

Diversity The tutorial brings together a diverse group of presenters, each with unique computer science and linguistics backgrounds, hailing from different institutions such as the University of Gothenburg, the Queen Mary University of London, the University of Milan and Vrije Universiteit Brussel. This diverse group of experts reflects the interdisciplinary nature of the research field, where knowledge from linguistic analysis and computational methodologies converge. Furthermore, the tutorial will showcase the rich linguistic diversity of studying LSC, covering several languages, including Russian, English, Swedish, Latin, Spanish, and Italian. Exploring multiple languages will give attendees insights into how semantic change manifests across language families, historical periods, and socio-cultural contexts. The tutorial aims to foster a global perspective on the diachronic change of word meanings by encompassing various languages, encouraging participants to draw parallels and distinctions between languages.

Audience size The proposed tutorial is expected to attract around 100+ attendees, motivated by the considerable interest and attendance observed in related events like the International Workshop on Computational Approaches to Historical Language Change and the Ever Evolving NLP (EvoNLP) Workshop.

Venue We prefer ACL 2024 and NAACL 2024 as our tutorial is tailored for an audience that includes linguists and computer scientists. EMNLP 2024 stands as our second preferred option. Should there be no available slots, we would consider EACL 2024.

Pedagogical material All materials, including presentations and Python notebooks, will be available online at the tutorial website: `https://www.changeiskey.org/event/2024-eacl-tutorial/`.

Past tutorials

- LREC 2022 Tutorial *Lexical Semantic Change: Models, Data and Evaluation*: While this tutorial primarily devoted its attention to resources for LSC Detection, our proposed tutorial aims to provide more comprehensive coverage on the subject of Computational Modeling of Semantic Change, as we will delve into a rich introduction of the linguistic aspects of semantic change, and a detailed exploration of computational models, emphasizing not just the conventional approaches, but also focusing extensively on the architectures of cutting-edge models.

5 Reading list

- Introduction to Semantic Change (Geeraerts et al., 2012; Traugott, 2017; Geeraerts, 2020)
- Surveys (Kutuzov et al., 2018; Tahmasebi et al., 2021; Montanelli and Periti, 2023)
- Benchmarks (Schlechtweg et al., 2020a; Basile et al., 2020c; Kutuzov and Pivovarova, 2021)
- Models (Hamilton et al., 2016c; Yao et al., 2018; Giulianelli et al., 2023; Cassotti et al., 2023; Periti et al., 2023)

6 Presenters

Nina Tahmasebi is an associate professor at the University of Gothenburg. She has researched computational methods for semantic change since 2008 and leads the *Change is Key!* program, a 6-year research program aimed at developing state-of-the-art methods for semantic change and use these to address research questions from historical linguistics as well as the humanities and social sciences. She is the chair of the LChange workshop series on Computational modeling for language change and has extensive experience in modeling and evaluation for semantic change.

Pierluigi Cassotti is a PhD student at the University of Bari (Italy) and a researcher at the University of Gothenburg (Sweden). He has been a co-organiser of the LREC 2022 Tutorial *Lexical Semantic Change: Models, Data and Evaluation*, a co-organiser of the *(LChange'23) Workshop*, and a co-organiser of the *DIACR-Ita shared task for the Italian language*. His research aims to fill the gap between Natural Language Processing tools and Diachronic Linguistics, focusing on developing models for LSCD and creating resources for the diachronic analysis of language.

Francesco Periti is a PhD student at the University of Milan (Italy). His research primarily centers around computational modeling of language change, with a specific focus on Lexical Semantic Change detection. He has been a co-organiser of the 4th International Workshop on Computational Approaches to Historical Language Change 2023 (LChange'23).

Stefano De Pascale is postdoctoral scholar at the KU Leuven (Belgium), as a member of the *Change is Key!* program, and assistant professor in Italian linguistics at the Vrije Universiteit Brussel (Belgium). He obtained his PhD in Linguistics in 2019 at the KU Leuven. In his dissertation he investigated the contribution of token-based vector space models in the study of lexical variation. In 2021 he obtained a junior FWO-postdoctoral fellowship to work on the computational modelling of diachronic prototype semantics.

Haim Dubossarsky is a lecturer for NLP at Queen Mary University of London. In his work, Haim emphasises the importance of careful methodological routines in using computational methods in NLP as a condition for reliable and validated scientific conclusions, and is a well-cited author in the field.

References

Yvonne Adesam, Dana Dannells, and Nina Tahmasebi. 2019. Exploring the Quality of the Digital Historical Newspaper Archive KubHist. In *Proceedings of the Digital Humanities in the Nordic Countries 4th Conference, DHN 2019, Copenhagen, Denmark, March 7-9, 2019.*, CEUR Workshop Proceedings. CEUR-WS.org.

Reem Alatrash, Dominik Schlechtweg, Jonas Kuhn, and Sabine Schulte im Walde. CCOHA: Clean corpus of historical american english. In *Proceedings of The 12th Language Resources and Evaluation Conference, LREC 2020*, pages 6958–6966. European Language Resources Association.

Nikolay Arefyev, Daniil Homskiy, Maksim Fedoseev, Adis Davletov, Vitaly Protasov, and Alexander Panchenko. 2021. DeepMistake: Which Senses are Hard to Distinguish for a WordinContext Model. In *Computational Linguistics and Intellectual Technologies - Papers from the Annual International Conference "Dialogue" 2021*, volume 2021-June. Section: 20.

Pierpaolo Basile, Annalina Caputo, Tommaso Caselli, Pierluigi Cassotti, and Rossella Varvara. 2020a. A Diachronic Italian Corpus based on "L'Unità". In *Proceedings of the Seventh Italian Conference on Computational Linguistics, CLiC-it 2020*, volume 2769 of *CEUR Workshop Proceedings*. CEUR-WS.org.

Pierpaolo Basile, Annalina Caputo, Tommaso Caselli, Pierluigi Cassotti, and Rossella Varvara. 2020b. Diacr-ita @ EVALITA2020: overview of the EVALITA2020 diachronic lexical semantics (diacr-ita) task. In *Proceedings of the Seventh Evaluation Campaign of Natural Language Processing and Speech Tools for Italian. Final Workshop (EVALITA 2020), Online event, December 17th, 2020*, volume 2765 of *CEUR Workshop Proceedings*. CEUR-WS.org.

Pierpaolo Basile, Annalina Caputo, Tommaso Caselli, Pierluigi Cassotti, and Rossella Varvara. 2020c. DIACR-Ita @ EVALITA2020: Overview of the EVALITA2020 Diachronic Lexical Semantics (DIACR-Ita) Task. In *Proceedings of the Seventh Evaluation Campaign of Natural Language Processing and Speech Tools for Italian. Final Workshop (EVALITA 2020)*, volume 2765 of *CEUR Workshop Proceedings*. CEUR-WS.org.

Pierpaolo Basile, Annalina Caputo, and Giovanni Semeraro. 2016. Temporal Random Indexing: a Tool for Analysing Word Meaning Variations in News. In *Proceedings of the First International Workshop on Recent Trends in News Information Retrieval co-located with 38th European Conference on Information Retrieval (ECIR 2016)*, volume 1568 of *CEUR Workshop Proceedings*, pages 39–41, Padua, Italy. CEUR-WS.org.

Pierpaolo Basile, Giovanni Semeraro, and Annalina Caputo. Kronos-it: a dataset for the italian semantic change detection task. In *Proceedings of the Sixth Italian Conference on Computational Linguistics*, volume 2481 of *CEUR Workshop Proceedings*. CEUR-WS.org.

Yuri Bizzoni, Stefania Degaetano-Ortlieb, Peter Fankhauser, and Elke Teich. 2020. Linguistic variation and change in 250 years of english scientific writing: A data-driven approach. *Frontiers in Artificial Intelligence*, 3.

Dallas Card. 2023. Substitution-based semantic change detection using contextual embeddings. In *Proceedings of the 61st Annual Meeting of the Association for Computational Linguistics (Volume 2: Short Papers)*, pages 590–602, Toronto, Canada. Association for Computational Linguistics.

Valerio Di Carlo, Federico Bianchi, and Matteo Palmonari. 2019. Training Temporal Word Embeddings with a Compass. In *The Thirty-Third AAAI Conference on Artificial Intelligence, AAAI 2019, The Thirty-First Innovative Applications of Artificial Intelligence Conference, IAAI 2019, The Ninth AAAI Symposium on Educational Advances in Artificial Intelligence, EAAI*, pages 6326–6334, Honolulu, Hawaii,USA. AAAI Press.

Pierluigi Cassotti, Pierpaolo Basile, Marco de Gemmis, and Giovanni Semeraro. 2020. Analyzing gaussian distribution of semantic shifts in lexical semantic change models. *IJCoL. Italian Journal of Computational Linguistics*, 6(6-2):23–36.

Pierluigi Cassotti, Lucia Siciliani, Marco DeGemmis, Giovanni Semeraro, and Pierpaolo Basile. 2023. XL-LEXEME: WiC pretrained model for cross-lingual LEXical sEMantic changE. In *Proceedings of the 61st Annual Meeting of the Association for Computational Linguistics (Volume 2: Short Papers)*, pages 1577–1585, Toronto, Canada. Association for Computational Linguistics.

Jing Chen, Emmanuele Chersoni, Dominik Schlechtweg, Jelena Prokic, and Chu-Ren Huang. 2023. ChiWUG: A Graph-based Evaluation Dataset for Chinese Lexical Semantic Change Detection. In *Proceedings of the 4th Workshop on Computational Approaches to Historical Language Change*, pages 93–99, Singapore. Association for Computational Linguistics.

Jacob Devlin, Ming-Wei Chang, Kenton Lee, and Kristina Toutanova. 2018. BERT: pre-training of deep bidirectional transformers for language understanding. *CoRR*, abs/1810.04805.

Haim Dubossarsky, Simon Hengchen, Nina Tahmasebi, and Dominik Schlechtweg. 2019. Time-Out: Temporal Referencing for Robust Modeling of Lexical Semantic Change. In *Proceedings of the 57th Conference of the Association for Computational Linguistics, ACL 2019, Volume 1: Long Papers*, pages 457–470, Florence, Italy. Association for Computational Linguistics.

Nikhil Garg, Londa Schiebinger, Dan Jurafsky, and James Zou. 2018. Word embeddings quantify 100 years of gender and ethnic stereotypes. *Proceedings of the National Academy of Sciences*, 115(16):E3635–E3644.

Dirk Geeraerts. 1997. *Diachronic Prototype Semantics: A Contribution to Historical Lexicology*. Clarendon Press, Oxford.

Dirk Geeraerts. 2020. Semantic change. "what the smurf?". In Daniel Gutzmann, Lisa Matthewson, Cécile Meier, Hotze Rullmann, and Thomas E. Zimmermann, editors, *The Wiley Blackwell Companion to Semantics*. Wiley Blackwell, Hoboken NJ.

Dirk Geeraerts, Caroline Gevaert, and Dirk Speelman. 2012. How anger rose: Hypothesis testing in diachronic semantics. In Kathryn Allan and Justyna Robinson, editors, *Current methods in historical semantics*, pages 73–109. De Gruyter Mouton, Berlin/New York.

Mario Giulianelli, Marco Del Tredici, and Raquel Fernández. 2020. Analysing lexical semantic change with contextualised word representations. In *Proceedings of the 58th Annual Meeting of the Association for Computational Linguistics*, pages 3960–3973, Online. Association for Computational Linguistics.

Mario Giulianelli, Iris Luden, Raquel Fernandez, and Andrey Kutuzov. 2023. Interpretable word sense representations via definition generation: The case of semantic change analysis. In *Proceedings of the 61st Annual Meeting of the Association for Computational Linguistics (Volume 1: Long Papers)*, pages 3130–3148, Toronto, Canada. Association for Computational Linguistics.

Thomas Haider and Steffen Eger. 2019. Semantic change and emerging tropes in a large corpus of New High German poetry. In *Proceedings of the 1st International Workshop on Computational Approaches to Historical Language Change*, pages 216–222, Florence, Italy. Association for Computational Linguistics.

William L. Hamilton, Jure Leskovec, and Dan Jurafsky. 2016a. Diachronic word embeddings reveal statistical laws of semantic change. In *54th Annual Meeting of the Association for Computational Linguistics, ACL 2016 - Long Papers*, volume 3, pages 1489–1501.

William L. Hamilton, Jure Leskovec, and Dan Jurafsky. 2016b. Diachronic Word Embeddings Reveal Statistical Laws of Semantic Change. In *Proceedings of the 54th Annual Meeting of the Association for Computational Linguistics, ACL 2016, Volume 1: Long Papers*, Berlin, Germany. The Association for Computer Linguistics.

William L. Hamilton, Jure Leskovec, and Dan Jurafsky. 2016c. Diachronic Word Embeddings Reveal Statistical Laws of Semantic Change. In *Proceedings of the 54th Annual Meeting of the Association for Computational Linguistics (Volume 1: Long Papers)*, pages 1489–1501, Berlin, Germany. Association for Computational Linguistics.

Andrey Kutuzov, Lilja Øvrelid, Terrence Szymanski, and Erik Velldal. 2018. Diachronic word embeddings and semantic shifts: a survey. In *Proceedings of the 27th International Conference on Computational Linguistics, COLING 2018*, pages 1384–1397, Santa Fe, New Mexico, USA. Association for Computational Linguistics.

Andrey Kutuzov and Lidia Pivovarova. 2021. RuShiftEval: A Shared Task on Semantic Shift Detection for Russian. In *Proc. of the International Conference on Computational Linguistics and Intellectual Technologies (Dialogue)*, 20, (online). Redkollegija sbornika.

Andrey Kutuzov, Lidia Pivovarova, and others. RuShiftEval: a shared task on semantic shift detection for russian. In *Computational linguistics and intellectual technologies: Papers from the annual conference Dialogue*. Redkollegija sbornika.

Andrey Kutuzov, Samia Touileb, Petter Mæhlum, Tita Ranveig Enstad, and Alexandra Wittemann. 2022. Nordiachange: Diachronic semantic change dataset for norwegian. In *Proceedings of the Thirteenth Language Resources and Evaluation Conference, LREC 2022, Marseille, France, 20-25 June 2022*, pages 2563–2572. European Language Resources Association.

Severin Laicher, Sinan Kurtyigit, Dominik Schlechtweg, Jonas Kuhn, and Sabine Schulte im Walde. 2021. Explaining and improving BERT performance on lexical semantic change detection. In *Proceedings of the 16th Conference of the European Chapter of the Association for Computational Linguistics: Student Research Workshop*, pages 192–202, Online. Association for Computational Linguistics.

Omer Levy and Yoav Goldberg. Neural Word Embedding as Implicit Matrix Factorization. In *Proc of NeurIPS*, volume 27. Curran Associates, Inc.

Bastien Liétard, Mikaela Keller, and Pascal Denis. 2023. A tale of two laws of semantic change: Predicting synonym changes with distributional semantic models. *CoRR*, abs/2305.19143.

Jani Marjanen, Lidia Pivovarova, Elaine Zosa, and Jussi Kurunmäki. 2019. Clustering ideological terms in historical newspaper data with diachronic word embeddings. In *5th International Workshop on Computational History, HistoInformatics@TPDL 2019, Oslo, Norway, September 12, 2019*, volume 2461 of *CEUR Workshop Proceedings*, pages 21–29. CEUR-WS.org.

Barbara McGillivray and Adam Kilgarriff. 2013. Tools for historical corpus research, and a corpus of Latin. In *New Methods in Historical Corpus Linguistics*, pages 247–257, Tübingen. Narr.

Tomás Mikolov, Kai Chen, Greg Corrado, and Jeffrey Dean. 2013. Efficient estimation of word representations in vector space. In *1st International Conference on Learning Representations, ICLR 2013, Workshop Track Proceedings*.

Stefano Montanelli and Francesco Periti. 2023. A Survey on Contextualised Semantic Shift Detection. *arXiv preprint arXiv:2304.01666*.

Roberto Navigli. 2009. Word Sense Disambiguation: A Survey. *ACM Comput. Surv.*, 41(2).

Francesco Periti, Alfio Ferrara, Stefano Montanelli, and Martin Ruskov. 2022. What is Done is Done: an Incremental Approach to Semantic Shift Detection. In *Proc. of LChange*, pages 33–43, Dublin, Ireland. ACL.

Francesco Periti, Sergio Picascia, Stefano Montanelli, Alfio Ferrara, and Nina Tahmasebi. 2023. Studying Word Meaning Evolution through Incremental Semantic Shift Detection: A Case Study of Italian Parliamentary Speeches.

Mohammad Taher Pilehvar and Jose Camacho-Collados. 2019. WiC: the Word-in-Context Dataset for Evaluating Context-Sensitive Meaning Representations. In *Proc. of the 2019 Conference of the North American Chapter of the Association for Computational Linguistics: Human Language Technologies, Volume 1 (Long and Short Papers)*, pages 1267–1273, Minneapolis, Minnesota. Association for Computational Linguistics.

Maxim Rachinskiy and Nikolay Arefyev. 2021. Zeroshot Crosslingual Transfer of a Gloss Language Model for Semantic Change Detection. In *Computational Linguistics and Intellectual Technologies - Papers from the Annual International Conference "Dialogue" 2021*, volume 2021-June. Section: 20.

Guy D. Rosin, Ido Guy, and Kira Radinsky. 2022. Time Masking for Temporal Language Models. In *WSDM '22: The Fifteenth ACM International Conference on Web Search and Data Mining, Virtual Event / Tempe, AZ, USA, February 21 - 25, 2022*, pages 833–841. ACM.

Guy D. Rosin and Kira Radinsky. 2022. Temporal Attention for Language Models. *CoRR*, abs/2202.02093.

Evan Sandhaus. 2008. The new york times annotated corpus. *Linguistic Data Consortium, Philadelphia*, 6(12):e26752.

Dominik Schlechtweg, Sabine Schulte im Walde, and Stefanie Eckmann. 2018. Diachronic Usage Relatedness (DURel): A Framework for the Annotation of Lexical Semantic Change. In *Proceedings of the 2018 Conference of the North American Chapter of the Association for Computational Linguistics: Human Language Technologies, NAACL-HLT, Volume 2 (Short Papers)*, pages 169–174, New Orleans, Louisiana, USA. Association for Computational Linguistics.

Dominik Schlechtweg, Barbara McGillivray, Simon Hengchen, Haim Dubossarsky, and Nina Tahmasebi. 2020a. SemEval-2020 Task 1: Unsupervised Lexical Semantic Change Detection. In *Proceedings of the Fourteenth Workshop on Semantic Evaluation, SemEval@COLING2020*, pages 1–23, Barcelona (online). International Committee for Computational Linguistics.

Dominik Schlechtweg, Barbara McGillivray, Simon Hengchen, Haim Dubossarsky, and Nina Tahmasebi. 2020b. SemEval-2020 Task 1: Unsupervised Lexical Semantic Change Detection. In *Proceedings of the Fourteenth Workshop on Semantic Evaluation, SemEval@COLING2020*, pages 1–23. International Committee for Computational Linguistics.

Gustaf Stern. 1921. *Swift, swiftly, and their synonyms: A contribution to semantic analysis and theory*, volume 23. Elanders boktr.

Terrence Szymanski. 2017. Temporal Word Analogies: Identifying Lexical Replacement with Diachronic Word Embeddings. In *Proceedings of the 55th Annual Meeting of the Association for Computational Linguistics, ACL 2017, Volume 2: Short Papers*, pages 448–453, Vancouver, Canada. Association for Computational Linguistics.

Nina Tahmasebi, Lars Borin, and Adam Jatowt. 2021. Survey of Computational Approaches to Lexical Semantic Change Detection.

Deutsches Textarchiv. Grundlage für ein referenzkorpus der neuhochdeutschen sprache. herausgegeben von der berlin-brandenburgischen akademie der wissenschaften.

Elizabeth Closs Traugott. 2017. Semantic change. In *Oxford Research Encyclopedia of Linguistics*.

Rocco Tripodi, Massimo Warglien, Simon Levis Sullam, and Deborah Paci. 2019. Tracing antisemitic language through diachronic embedding projections: France 1789-1914. In *Proceedings of the 1st International Workshop on Computational Approaches to Historical Language Change*, pages 115–125, Florence, Italy. Association for Computational Linguistics.

Ekaterina Vylomova, Sean Murphy, and Nicholas Haslam. 2019. Evaluation of semantic change of harm-related concepts in psychology. In *Proceedings of the 1st International Workshop on Computational Approaches to Historical Language Change*, pages 29–34, Florence, Italy. Association for Computational Linguistics.

Melvin Wevers. 2019. Using word embeddings to examine gender bias in Dutch newspapers, 1950-1990. In *Proceedings of the 1st International Workshop on Computational Approaches to Historical Language Change*, pages 92–97, Florence, Italy. Association for Computational Linguistics.

Zijun Yao, Yifan Sun, Weicong Ding, Nikhil Rao, and Hui Xiong. 2018. Dynamic Word Embeddings for Evolving Semantic Discovery. In *Proceedings of the Eleventh ACM International Conference on Web Search and Data Mining, WSDM 2018*, pages 673–681, Marina Del Rey, CA, USA. ACM.

Frank D. Zamora-Reina, Felipe Bravo-Marquez, and Dominik Schlechtweg. 2022. LSCDiscovery: A Shared Task on Semantic Change Discovery and Detection in Spanish. In *Proc. of the Workshop on Computational Approaches to Historical Language Change (LChange)*, pages 149–164, Dublin, Ireland. Association for Computational Linguistics (ACL).

Berliner Zeitung. Diachronic newspaper corpus published by staatsbibliothek zu berlin.

Item Response Theory for Natural Language Processing

John P. Lalor,[1] Pedro Rodriguez,[2] João Sedoc,[3,4] Jose Hernandez-Orallo[5]
[1] IT, Analytics, and Operations, University of Notre Dame
[2] Meta FAIR, Seattle
[3] Technology, Operations and Statistics, New York University
[4] Center for Data Science, New York University
[5] Universitat Politècnica de València
john.lalor@nd.edu, me@pedro.ai, jsedoc@stern.nyu.edu, jorallo@upv.es

1 Description

This tutorial will introduce the NLP community to Item Response Theory (IRT; Baker, 2001). IRT is a method from the field of psychometrics for model and dataset assessment. IRT has been used for decades to build test sets for human subjects and estimate latent characteristics of dataset examples. Recently, there has been an uptick in work applying IRT to tasks in NLP. It is our goal to introduce the wider NLP community to IRT and show its benefits for a number of NLP tasks. From this tutorial, we hope to encourage wider adoption of IRT among NLP researchers.

As NLP models improve in performance and increase in complexity, new methods for evaluation are needed to appropriately evaluate performance improvements. In addition, data quality continues to be important. Models exploitation of annotation artifacts, annotation errors, and a misalignment between models and dataset difficulty can hinder an appropriate assessment of model performance. As models reach and exceed human performance on certain tasks, it gets more difficult to distinguish between improvements and innovations and changes in scores due to chance. In this **three-hour, introductory** tutorial, we will review the current state of evaluation in NLP, then introduce IRT as a tool for NLP researchers to use when evaluating their data and models. We will also introduce and demonstrate the py-irt Python package for IRT model-fitting to help encourage adoption and facilitate IRT use.

We believe that this should be a tutorial instead of a specialized workshop since the tutorial will aid in exposing a larger NLP audience to IRT. While this methodology has been applied successfully to NLP applications, further community exposure specifically for graduate students may provide a new methodological perspective. We aim to make the tutorial interactive with hands-on Jupyter notebooks which will give concrete simple examples. Tutorial materials are available online.[1]

2 Target Audience/Prerequisites

The tutorial content will be self-contained so that a broad target audience of *CL conference attendees (researchers, PhD students, industry professionals, etc.) can take away information on incorporating IRT in their workflow. In terms of prerequisites, we expect the audience to have basic knowledge of probability and statistics. We also expect audience members to have experience with Python is useful for py-irt.

3 Outline

1. Evaluation in NLP (30 minutes)
2. Introduction to IRT (1 hour)
    - Defining IRT Models
    - IRT Model Fitting
    - Introduction to py-irt
        - This section will include tutorial content and live demonstration of the py-irt package.
3. IRT in NLP (45 minutes)
    - Building Test Sets
        - Model Evaluation
        - Chatbot Evaluation
    - Training Dynamics
        - Example Mining
        - Curriculum Learning
    - Model and Data Evaluation
        - Rethinking Leaderboards
        - Features Related to Difficulty
4. Advanced Topics and Opportunities for Future Work (45 minutes)

[1] https://eacl2024irt.github.io/

Proceedings of the 18th Conference of the European Chapter of the Association for Computational Linguistics Tutorial Abstracts, pages 9–13

3.1 Evaluation in NLP

Today more than ever evaluation of generative AI and datasets has become more important than ever. We will start with a brief introduction to evaluation in NLP, covering the state of the field over the years (Church and Hestness, 2019). We will cover traditional classification metrics, the rise of leaderboards (Ethayarajh and Jurafsky, 2020), and issues with incremental improvement on summary statistics (Blum and Hardt, 2015).

3.2 Introduction to IRT

We will then move to an introduction of IRT (Baker, 2001; Carlson and von Davier, 2013). IRT is a psychometric method for estimating latent characteristics of test takers and test examples (typically called "items"). IRT has a rich history in the psychometric literature, and is used to construct tests of subject competency (Carlson and von Davier, 2013), mental health screeners (Cole et al., 2011), and health literacy tests (Lalor et al., 2018a), among others.

As IRT is most likely new to the NLP audience, we will spend time discussing the motivation for IRT and the mathematical foundations which make the building blocks of IRT models. We will introduce IRT, highlight some of the important use cases from the literature, and introduce the relevant IRT models.

Specifically, we will introduce models that are used when there is a known correct answer, e.g., an NLP classification task. Such models take a binarized data input and estimate the latent ability ("skill") of the subject and the latent parameters (such as difficulty) of the dataset items.

We will describe how these models are fit, and highlight issues with traditional methods when considering NLP datasets. Traditionally, sampling methods have been use to fit IRT models, but they are computationally expensive on today's large-scale datasets (Wu et al., 2020). We will then introduce variational-inference methods (VI) for IRT model fitting and show how they can alleviate some of the prior concerns (Natesan et al., 2016; Lalor et al., 2019; Wu et al., 2020).

Lastly, we will introduce the py-irt package for fitting IRT models in Python (Lalor and Rodriguez, 2022) and demonstrate how the tool is used using Jupyter notebooks. While IRT has shown promise in NLP, existing software for fitting models are limited by human-data sized constraints. The py-irt package leverages variational-inference (VI) methods to fit IRT models fast and with large data sets. This section of the tutorial will cover the methods built into py-irt and also include a demo with Jupyter notebooks of using py-irt for different NLP evaluation tasks.

3.3 IRT for NLP

We will next discuss how IRT can and has been incorporated into NLP. Prior work has looked at building new test sets with IRT, conducting human-machine comparisons, reevaluating leaderboards, and evaluating chatbot outputs, among other tasks.

3.3.1 IRT for NLP: Dataset Construction and Evaluation

We will first look at IRT for NLP dataset construction and analysis (Lalor et al., 2016; Martínez-Plumed et al., 2019; Sedoc and Ungar, 2020). Specifically, how can one use IRT to build a test set with a variety of examples included that can measure a range of model ability. We will show how IRT can complement traditional evaluation metrics while also revealing new information about both models and test data (Vania et al., 2021; Amidei et al., 2020).

3.3.2 IRT for NLP: Training Dynamics

Next, we will show how IRT can be used to improve the model training process. For example, by filtering datasets to exclude outliers (e.g., those examples that are too easy or too hard) or by using IRT to build a curriculum learning pipeline (Lalor and Yu, 2020), model training can be done more effectively and with better results.

3.3.3 IRT for NLP: Model Evaluation

Finally, we will discuss how IRT can help us to reimagine model evaluation (Otani et al., 2016; Sedoc and Ungar, 2020). We will show how incorporating IRT into leaderboards can give us much more information on model performance (Rodriguez et al., 2021). We will also show how targeted model probing using IRT can lead to new insights about model behavior (Lalor et al., 2018b; Laverghetta Jr. et al., 2021). Finally, we will compare IRT to other methods such as Elo-Ranking, TrueSkill, and other methods.

3.3.4 Advanced Topics

Lastly, we will discuss opportunities for further incorporating IRT into NLP research. This section will discuss more advanced IRT models, as well as ways that NLP research can inform IRT.

For example, what characteristics of examples make them more difficult (Rodriguez et al., 2022)? Also, we will cover IRT extensions and variants to parametrize new instances, such as proxies for difficulty (Martínez-Plumed et al., 2022), or using language models to annotate instance demands, the use of the agent characteristic curves (Martinez-Plumed and Hernandez-Orallo, 2018; Hernández-Orallo et al., 2021) and other ways to use IRT in cases where there is no population of systems.

3.4 Content Breadth

Our goal in this tutorial is to introduce the audience to IRT broadly, and the applications of IRT in NLP specifically. To that end, the content we present will be a mix of foundational IRT research and methods from psychometrics, recent work by the presenters, and work from others in the NLP community who have incorporated IRT into their research.

4 Diversity Considerations

The presenters represent a mix of industry and academic researchers. We also span both Europe and the US. The methods described can be applied to a variety of NLP tasks and languages. The tutorial content will be posted online for wide distribution beyond those able to attend the conference.

5 Ethics Statement

IRT methods can provide fine-grained information about dataset examples and models. With regard to datasets, IRT can potentially surface discrepancies in how groups of examples are handled by NLP models. For example, IRT analyses may show that examples collected from a certain demographic group are systematically more difficult than those examples collected from another demographic group.

6 Pedagogy

We hope that this tutorial can serve as a comprehensive introduction to IRT for an NLP audience and that the content can be reused by others who are not able to attend. To that end, the tutorial will include a combination of presentation slides, demos via Jupyter Notebooks, and interactive sessions in Jupyter notebooks. All content for the tutorial will be hosted online and made publicly available for future use and dissemination.

7 Presenters

John P. Lalor is an Assistant Professor of IT, Analytics, and Operations at the University of Notre Dame. His research interests include model evaluation, curriculum learning, fairness, and BioNLP. Prior to Notre Dame, John received his PhD in Computer Science from the University of Massachusetts, Amherst (advised by Hong Yu) in 2020. John has presented a tutorial on Evaluation and Interpretability in Deep Neural Networks to the 2018 American Medical Informatics Association (AMIA) Annual Symposium with Abhyuday Jagannatha and Hong Yu. Website: `https://jplalor.github.io/`.

Pedro Rodriguez is a researcher at Meta AI – FAIR. His research interests include question answering, information retrieval, and evaluation. Before joining Meta, Rodriguez completed his PhD at the University of Maryland, advised by Jordan Boyd-Graber. He has reviewed for ACL conferences and workshops, area chaired for COLING, was an organizer of the Dynamic Adversarial Data Collection Workshop at NAACL 2022, and an organizer of a question answering challenge at NeurIPS 2017. Website: `https://www.pedro.ai/`.

João Sedoc is an Assistant Professor in the department of Technology, Operations and Statistics at New York University Stern School of Business. He is also affiliated with the Center for Data Science at New York University and one of the co-PIs of the Machine Learning for Language (ML^2) group. João's research areas are at the intersection of machine learning and natural language processing. His interests include conversational agents, model evaluation, deep learning, crowdsourcing, spectral clustering, and time series analysis. He has organized multiple workshops: Workshop on Insights from Negative Results in NLP (EMNLP 2020-2021, ACL 2022, EACL 2023), the Workshop on Chatbots and Conversational Agent Technologies & Dialogue Breakdown Detection Challenge (DBDC) (IWSDS 2019, 2020, 2021), Workshop on Neural Conversational AI (ICLR 2021), Workshop on Computational Approaches to Subjectivity, Sentiment and Social Media Analysis (2021-3), Dialog System Technology Challenge Tracks (AAAI 2021, SIGDIAL 2023), GEM workshop (EMNLP 2023), HumEval workshop 2023 (RANNLP 2023) Website: `https://www.stern.nyu.edu/faculty/bio/joao-sedoc`.

Jose Hernandez-Orallo is Professor at the Universitat Politècnica de València and Senior Research Fellow at the Leverhulme Centre for the Future of Intelligence, University of Cambridge, UK. His academic and research activities have spanned several areas of AI, machine learning, data science and intelligence measurement, with a focus on a more insightful analysis of the capabilities, generality, progress, impact and risks of AI. He has published five books and more than two hundred journal articles and conference papers on these topics. His research in the area of machine intelligence evaluation has been covered by several popular outlets, such as The Economist, New Scientist and Nature. For a couple of decades, he has vindicated a more integrated view of the evaluation of natural and artificial intelligence, a position represented by his book "The Measure of All Minds" (Cambridge University Press, 2017, PROSE Award 2018) and by multiple papers and events, using IRT, extensions and techniques from some other disciplines to evaluate general-purpose AI such as LLMs. He is a member of AAAI, CLAIRE and ELLIS, and a EurAI Fellow. Website: `https://josephorallo.webs.upv.es/`

8 Estimate Audience Size

We expect between 50 to 150 attendees. This is based on previous experience at *CL tutorials as well as interest from others to learn about IRT methods.

References

Jacopo Amidei, Paul Piwek, and Alistair Willis. 2020. Identifying annotator bias: A new IRT-based method for bias identification. In *Proceedings of the 28th International Conference on Computational Linguistics*, pages 4787–4797, Barcelona, Spain (Online). International Committee on Computational Linguistics.

Frank B Baker. 2001. *The basics of item response theory*. ERIC.

Avrim Blum and Moritz Hardt. 2015. The ladder: A reliable leaderboard for machine learning competitions. PMLR.

James E Carlson and Matthias von Davier. 2013. Item response theory. *ETS Research Report Series*, 2013(2):i–69.

Kenneth Ward Church and Joel Hestness. 2019. A survey of 25 years of evaluation. *Natural Language Engineering*, 25(6):753–767.

David A Cole, Li Cai, Nina C Martin, Robert L Findling, Eric A Youngstrom, Judy Garber, John F Curry, Janet S Hyde, Marilyn J Essex, Bruce E Compas, et al. 2011. Structure and measurement of depression in youths: applying item response theory to clinical data. *Psychological assessment*, 23(4):819.

Kawin Ethayarajh and Dan Jurafsky. 2020. Utility is in the eye of the user: A critique of NLP leaderboards. Association for Computational Linguistics.

José Hernández-Orallo, Bao Sheng Loe, Lucy Cheke, Fernando Martínez-Plumed, and Seán Ó hÉigeartaigh. 2021. General intelligence disentangled via a generality metric for natural and artificial intelligence. *Scientific reports*, 11(1):22822.

John P. Lalor and Pedro Rodriguez. 2022. py-irt: A scalable item response theory library for python. *INFORMS Journal on Computing*.

John P. Lalor, Hao Wu, Li Chen, Kathleen M. Mazor, and Hong Yu. 2018a. ComprehENotes, an Instrument to Assess Patient Reading Comprehension of Electronic Health Record Notes: Development and Validation. *Journal of Medical Internet Research*, 20(4):e139.

John P. Lalor, Hao Wu, Tsendsuren Munkhdalai, and Hong Yu. 2018b. Understanding deep learning performance through an examination of test set difficulty: A psychometric case study. In *Proceedings of the 2018 Conference on Empirical Methods in Natural Language Processing*, pages 4711–4716, Brussels, Belgium. Association for Computational Linguistics.

John P. Lalor, Hao Wu, and Hong Yu. 2016. Building an evaluation scale using item response theory. In *Proceedings of the 2016 Conference on Empirical Methods in Natural Language Processing*, pages 648–657, Austin, Texas. Association for Computational Linguistics.

John P. Lalor, Hao Wu, and Hong Yu. 2019. Learning latent parameters without human response patterns: Item response theory with artificial crowds. In *Proceedings of the 2019 Conference on Empirical Methods in Natural Language Processing and the 9th International Joint Conference on Natural Language Processing (EMNLP-IJCNLP)*, pages 4249–4259, Hong Kong, China. Association for Computational Linguistics.

John P. Lalor and Hong Yu. 2020. Dynamic data selection for curriculum learning via ability estimation. In *Findings of the Association for Computational Linguistics: EMNLP 2020*, pages 545–555, Online. Association for Computational Linguistics.

Antonio Laverghetta Jr., Animesh Nighojkar, Jamshidbek Mirzakhalov, and John Licato. 2021. Can transformer language models predict psychometric properties? In *Proceedings of *SEM 2021: The Tenth Joint Conference on Lexical and Computational Semantics*, pages 12–25, Online. Association for Computational Linguistics.

Fernando Martínez-Plumed, David Castellano, Carlos Monserrat-Aranda, and José Hernández-Orallo. 2022. When ai difficulty is easy: The explanatory power of predicting irt difficulty. In *Proceedings of the AAAI Conference on Artificial Intelligence*, volume 36, pages 7719–7727.

Fernando Martinez-Plumed and Jose Hernandez-Orallo. 2018. Dual indicators to analyze ai benchmarks: Difficulty, discrimination, ability, and generality. *IEEE Transactions on Games*, 12(2):121–131.

Fernando Martínez-Plumed, Ricardo BC Prudêncio, Adolfo Martínez-Usó, and José Hernández-Orallo. 2019. Item response theory in ai: Analysing machine learning classifiers at the instance level. *Artificial intelligence*, 271:18–42.

Prathiba Natesan, Ratna Nandakumar, Tom Minka, and Jonathan D Rubright. 2016. Bayesian prior choice in irt estimation using mcmc and variational bayes. *Frontiers in psychology*, 7:1422.

Naoki Otani, Toshiaki Nakazawa, Daisuke Kawahara, and Sadao Kurohashi. 2016. IRT-based aggregation model of crowdsourced pairwise comparison for evaluating machine translations. In *Proceedings of the 2016 Conference on Empirical Methods in Natural Language Processing*, pages 511–520, Austin, Texas. Association for Computational Linguistics.

Pedro Rodriguez, Joe Barrow, Alexander Miserlis Hoyle, John P. Lalor, Robin Jia, and Jordan Boyd-Graber. 2021. Evaluation examples are not equally informative: How should that change NLP leaderboards? In *Proceedings of the 59th Annual Meeting of the Association for Computational Linguistics and the 11th International Joint Conference on Natural Language Processing (Volume 1: Long Papers)*, pages 4486–4503, Online. Association for Computational Linguistics.

Pedro Rodriguez, Phu Mon Htut, John Lalor, and João Sedoc. 2022. Clustering examples in multi-dataset benchmarks with item response theory. In *Proceedings of the Third Workshop on Insights from Negative Results in NLP*, pages 100–112, Dublin, Ireland. Association for Computational Linguistics.

João Sedoc and Lyle Ungar. 2020. Item response theory for efficient human evaluation of chatbots. In *Proceedings of the First Workshop on Evaluation and Comparison of NLP Systems*, pages 21–33, Online. Association for Computational Linguistics.

Clara Vania, Phu Mon Htut, William Huang, Dhara Mungra, Richard Yuanzhe Pang, Jason Phang, Haokun Liu, Kyunghyun Cho, and Samuel R. Bowman. 2021. Comparing test sets with item response theory. In *Proceedings of the 59th Annual Meeting of the Association for Computational Linguistics and the 11th International Joint Conference on Natural Language Processing (Volume 1: Long Papers)*, pages 1141–1158, Online. Association for Computational Linguistics.

M Wu, R Davis, B Domingue, C Piech, and Noah D Goodman. 2020. Variational item response theory: Fast, accurate, and expressive.

Language + Molecules

Carl Edwards and **Qingyun Wang** and **Heng Ji**
University of Illinois Urbana-Champaign
{cne2, qingyun4, hengji}@illinois.edu

1 Description

Climate change, access to food and water, pandemics— these words, when uttered, immediately summon to mind global challenges with possible disastrous outcomes. The world faces enormous problems in the coming decades on scales of complexity never-before-seen. To address these issues, developing scientific solutions which are scalable, flexible, and inexpensive is critical. Further, we need to develop these solutions quickly. Broadly speaking, chemistry can provide molecular solutions to many of these problems: breakthrough drugs (e.g., kinase inhibitors (Ferguson and Gray, 2018)), materials (e.g., organic photovoltaics (Kippelen et al., 2009)), and chemical processes. The extremely large search spaces in which these solutions exist make AI tools critical for finding them. Of particular note, multimodal models combining language with molecules are poised to be a critical tool for discovering these solutions (Zhang et al., 2023). In this tutorial, we will discuss the role which natural language processing can play in discovering and accelerating solutions to global problems via the broad chemistry domain.

One of the first questions that probably comes to mind is why we would want to integrate natural language with molecules. Succinctly, combining these types of information has the possibility to accelerate scientific discovery. As motivating scenarios, imagine a future where a doctor can receive a novel, patient-specific drug necessary to treat an ailment just by writing a few sentences describing the patient's symptoms (also taking into account their genotype, phenotype, and medical history). Or, imagine a scientist tackling challenging problems by designing a molecule satisfying desired functions (e.g., antimalarial or a photovoltaic) rather than its structure or low level properties (e.g., solubility). Controlling molecules and drug design in such a high-level manner has potential to be hugely impactful, but it requires a method of abstract description; luckily, humans have already developed one: natural language.

In recent months, because of this potential impact, significant attention and growth has occurred in scientific NLP and AI research, including integration of molecules with natural language and multimodal AI for science/medicine ((Zhang et al., 2023) Section 10.3.3, (Wang et al., 2023)). We believe a sufficient amount of work has now been done, along with significant interest generated, to propose an **Introductory to NLP** (yet still **Cutting-Edge**) tutorial on "Language + Molecules". This tutorial is designed to require no knowledge and will enable participants to begin exploring relevant and impactful research. Since most relevant work is still cutting-edge, this will broaden the community's understanding of the associated challenges, methodologies, and goals in multimodal molecule-language models. We will present an interactive hands-on example and release accompanying relevant code and resources. The tutorial will precede and prepare the way for the Language+Molecules workshop later in the year at ACL.

2 Outline [180 min.]

Applying language models to the scientific domain is becoming increasingly popular due to its potential impact for accelerating scientific discovery (Hope et al., 2022). Beyond extracting information from scientific literature, NLP has the possibility to increase control of the scientific discovery process, which can be achieved through multimodal representations and generative language models.

2.1 Background [60 min.]

Scientific Information Extraction [15 min.]

To start, we will provide a high-level overview on traditional NLP tasks used for scientific discovery (e.g., named entity recognition, entity linking, and relation extraction), as well as recent domain-specific LLMs designed for superior performance

Proceedings of the 18th Conference of the European Chapter of the Association for Computational Linguistics
Tutorial Abstracts, pages 14–20
March 21, 2024

on scientific tasks (Beltagy et al., 2019).

What is a molecule? [15 min.]

Half of the title is molecules, but what is one? We will start from scratch and discuss what a molecule actually is, including the basic constituents of molecules, atoms and bonds, and how they essentially form graph structures. Then, we will focus on molecular string languages, which are a key building block for chemical language models. We will discuss tradeoffs of these languages (Grisoni, 2023; Weininger, 1988; O'Boyle and Dalke, 2018; Krenn et al., 2020; Cheng et al., 2023). Krenn et al. (2020) proposes a formal grammar approach, which may particularly interest the ACL community.

Molecule Design using Language Models [15]

Now that we know what a molecule is, we will overview recent work applying NLP techniques to these molecular languages with impressive results. These molecular LLMs are trained with adapted pre-training techniques from (natural) language models to learn molecule representation from large collections of molecule strings (Frey et al., 2022; Chithrananda et al., 2020; Ahmad et al., 2022; Fabian et al., 2020; Schwaller et al., 2021; NVIDIA Corporation, 2022; Flam-Shepherd and Aspuru-Guzik, 2023; Tysinger et al., 2023). Applications include molecule and material generation, property prediction, and protein binding site prediction.

Drug Discovery–A Brief Primer [15 min.]

Ok, so NLP is being used for molecules now. What can we do with it?—here, we present a brief overview of drug discovery–an important but challenging problem. Historically, molecular discovery has commonly been done by humans who design and build individual molecules, but this can cost over a billion dollars and take over ten years (Gaudelet et al., 2021). We'll discuss a little of the process here, including non-NLP deep learning methods, so that we know how to improve it.

2.2 Integrating Language with Molecules [95]

What does natural language have to offer? [15]

At least at first, integrating languages and molecules seems like an odd idea. Here, we'll start an interactive discussion with the audience on what they think potential benefits might be. We'll make sure to mention the following major advantages, as discussed in the recent survey (Zhang et al., 2023):

1. **Generative Modeling**: One of the largest problems in current LLMs—-hallucination—becomes a strength for discovering molecules with high-level functions and abstract properties. In particular, language is compositional by nature (Szabó, 2020; Partee et al., 1984; Han et al., 2023), and therefore holds promise for composing these high-level properties (e.g., antimalarial) (Liu et al., 2022).
2. **Bridging Modalities**: Language can serve to "bridge" between modalities for scarce data.
3. **Domain Understanding**: Grounding language models into external real world knowledge (here, molecular structures) can improve understanding of unseen molecules and advance many emerging tasks, such as experimental procedure planning, which use LLMs as scientific agents.
4. **Democratization**: Language enables scientists without computational expertise to leverage advances in scientific AI.

Do I want multimodality? [5 min.]

An important, yet often overlooked, question in multimodal NLP is to ask: do I need multimodality? For example, if one wants to extract reactions from the literature, a text-to-text model (Vaucher et al., 2020) might be sufficient. However, editing a drug with high-level instructions requires language (Liu et al., 2023a; Fang et al., 2023). Here, we will dive into this question and discuss example scenarios with the audience for how to answer it.

2.2.1 Integrating Modalities [30 min.]

Ok, we've decided we want or need multimodality. Next, we need to discuss how people are currently tackling this-we'll start with two primary methods, bi-encoder models and joint representation models.

Bi-Encoder Models (and beyond) Bi-encoder models consist of an encoder branch for text and a branch for molecules. They have the advantage of not requiring direct, early integration of the two modalities, allowing existing single-modal models to be integrated. Representative examples we will discuss include Text2Mol (Edwards et al., 2021), CLAMP (Seidl et al., 2023), and BioTranslator (Xu et al., 2023). Generally, bi-encoder models are effective for cross-modal retrieval (Edwards et al., 2021; Su et al., 2022; Liu et al., 2022; Zhao et al., 2023b), but they may also be integrated into molecule (Su et al., 2022; Liu et al., 2022) and protein (Liu et al., 2023b) generation frameworks.

We'll talk about all these tasks, applications, and return to some important motivations (e.g., bridging modalities).

Joint Molecule-Language Models Joint models, on the other hand, seeks to model interactions between multiple modalities inside the same network to allow fine-grained interaction. We will discuss encoder-only models (Zeng et al., 2022), encoder-decoder models (Christofidellis et al., 2023), and decoder-only models (Liu et al., 2023c).
Model Differences: We will answer important questions such as: Which model should I use? What tasks can each do? Tasks include retrieval (Edwards et al., 2021), "translation" between molecules and language (Edwards et al., 2022a), editing molecules (Liu et al., 2022), and chemical reaction planning (Vaucher et al., 2020, 2021).

An Interactive Example - Targeting Microtubules for Cancer Treatment [20 min.]

At this point, there's been a lot of ideas thrown around. We'll consolidate them by exploring an interactive example of language-enabled molecule design using Google Colab.
We will focus on microtubules for the example. These cellular structures play an important role in many processes such cell growth and division, and mutations can be oncogenic (Mukhtar et al., 2014; Wattanathamsan and Pongrakhananon, 2022). In modern medicine, tumors such as pancreatic cancer are commonly treated by microtubule-targeting drugs such as paclitaxel (Albahde et al., 2021). In our example, we will explore creating new drugs with this function using natural language instructions, which may be useful in cases of paclitaxel resistance (Kavallaris, 2010). Our hands-on example will consist of three components:

1. **Language-enabled Drug Design:**
   Participants will explore inputs to language→molecule models to generate candidate drugs which target microtubules.
2. **Language-Guided Assay Testing:**
   Here, participants will test their proposed drugs in an assay. We will follow (Seidl et al., 2023), where natural language descriptions are used for assay predictions.
3. **Interaction Prediction:**
   Finally, we will test if proposed drugs bind with beta-tubulin using Autodock Vina, a well established docking program (Trott and Olson, 2010), via DockString (García-Ortegón et al., 2022).

Applications [25 min.] Here, we will discuss important applications to improve cross-discipline communication, including drug discovery (Mukhtar et al., 2014; Ferguson and Gray, 2018), organic photovoltaics (Kippelen et al., 2009), and catalyst discovery for renewable energy (Zitnick et al., 2020).

2.3 Recent Trends and Conclusion [25 min.]

Instruction-Following Molecular Design [10]

In the last year, instruction-following language models (Wei et al., 2021) have surged in popularity. Following this trend, training methodologies and datasets have recently emerged to allow language models to follow instructions related to molecule properties (Liang et al., 2023; Fang et al., 2023; Zeng et al., 2023; Zhao et al., 2023a). We will give a brief overview of this new line of work.

LLMs as Scientific Agents [5 min.] Further, we'll focus on recent work which looks to control experiments with language models (Boiko et al., 2023) and to create tools for enabling domain-specific capabilities in general language models (Bran et al., 2023; Liu et al., 2023a).

Conclusion [10 min.] We will discuss the key difficulties in the molecule-language domain that need to be addressed by the research community to allow similar progress to the vision-language domain. This includes 1) data scarcity due to domain expertise requirements, 2) addressing inconsistency when training on scientific literature, 3) improved methods for integrating geometric structures into LLMs, and 4) developing better evaluation metrics for chemical predictions without real-world experiments.

3 Logistics and Details

Diversity Considerations For this tutorial, our team originates from geographically distant countries and has varying level of seniority, including two PhD students and a full professor, The team includes a female researcher. This tutorial will augment a workshop on "Language + Molecules" to be held at a the ACL conference, which already has confirmed speakers and organizers with diversity in geography, ethnicity, and gender. This tutorial will strongly promote academic diversity, since it requires combining the specialties of chemists, physicians, pharmacists, computational linguists, and machine learning researchers. Further, this tutorial will promote the usage of NLP in high-impact areas, ranging from drug discovery to organic photovoltaics. The methods we will introduce are language-agnostic. All tutorial materials (slides, example, reading list) will be shared to reach such a diverse audience.

Target Audience and Background We will target this tutorial at NLP researchers with no knowledge of chemistry or molecules– thus, we will provide an extensive discussion of background material. However, we will assume that the target audience is familiar with modern NLP methods includ ing training deep neural network-based language models (e.g., BERT). We anticipate an audience size of 75-150 researchers. We will discuss relevant background for applying NLP to molecules and important applications in chemistry.

Reading List

- Molecule Representations and Language Models: (Weininger, 1988; Krenn et al., 2020; Cheng et al., 2023; Chithrananda et al., 2020; Ahmad et al., 2022; Tysinger et al., 2023)
- Molecule-Language Modeling: (Edwards et al., 2021; Zhao et al., 2023b; Zeng et al., 2022; Edwards et al., 2022b; Zhao et al., 2023a; Su et al., 2022; Liu et al., 2022, 2023c; Xu et al., 2023; Liu et al., 2023a; Luo et al., 2023)
- Applications: (Jordan and Roughley, 2009; Mukhtar et al., 2014; Kippelen et al., 2009)
- LLMs as Scientific Agents: (Boiko et al., 2023; Bran et al., 2023; Castro Nascimento and Pimentel, 2023; White et al., 2023)
- Survey: (Zhang et al., 2023) Section 10.3.3

We won't require reading these beforehand to ensure the tutorial is introductory.

Breadth of Tutorial Papers in the reading list were created by a diverse set of authors and include other disciplines. Specifically, only 2 papers and a survey from the instructors will be covered.

Ethical Considerations

Broader Impacts Our tutorial will have potential broader impacts: 1) It will help ACL researchers to better understand the research goals and constraints in chemical sciences, allowing them to do more impactful research there. 2) Studying language models in the context of non-human languages can help develop an understanding of their workings; due to our own personal linguistic biases, human researchers often misattribute abilities to language models. This is particularly relevant for developing new methodologies which are applicable to low-resource human languages. 3) It will promote further research in text-based molecule generation, with potential to enable a large shift in chemistry research so that custom molecules can be developed for each application or patient.

Ethical Concerns Like most methodologies reliant on LLMs, there may be biases learned by the model due to its large-scale training data. In this domain, these biases may affect what type of molecules are generated. Thus, any molecules or drugs discovered should be strictly evaluated by standard clinical processes before being considered for human or medicinal use. Another risk is that potentially dangerous molecules may be discovered. However, knowledge of dangerous molecule's existence and structure is generally not harmful due to the requisite technical knowledge and laboratory resources required for synthesis. Overall, we believe these downsides are outweighed by the benefits to the research and pharmaceutical communities.

3.1 Tutorial Presenters

Carl Edwards is a Ph.D. student in the Computer Science Department at UIUC. Broadly, he is interested in information extraction, information retrieval, text mining, representation learning, AI4Science, and multimodality. Particularly, he is interested in applying these to the scientific domain to accelerate scientific discovery. His work focuses on integrating natural language and molecules, especially using multimodal representations.

Qingyun Wang is a Ph.D. student in computer science at UIUC. His research lies in NLP for scientific discovery. Recently, he works on extracting reaction information from scientific literature. He served as a PC member in conferences including ICML, ACL, ICLR, NeurIPS, etc. His work was recognized in the first Alexa Prize competition and by the NAACL-HLT 2021 Best Demo Award. He has presented a tutorial at EMNLP 2021.

Heng Ji is a professor at the Computer Science Department of UIUC, and Amazon Scholar. She is a leading expert on multimodal multilingual information extraction, including NLP for Science with a particular interest in leveraging NLP for drug discovery. She has coordinated the NIST TAC Knowledge Base Population task since 2010. She has served as the PC Co-Chair of many conferences including NAACL-HLT2018 and AACL-IJCNLP2022 and has presented many tutorials. She was elected as NAACL secretary 2020-2023.

Acknowledgements

This work is supported by the Molecule Maker Lab Institute: an AI research institute program supported by NSF under award No. 2019897, and by the DOE Center for Advanced Bioenergy and Bioproducts Innovation, U.S. Department of Energy, Office of Science, Office of Biological and Environmental Research under Award Number DESC0018420. The views and conclusions contained herein are those of the authors and should not be interpreted as necessarily representing the official policies, either expressed or implied of, the National Science Foundation, the U.S. Department of Energy, and the U.S. Government. The U.S. Government is authorized to reproduce and distribute reprints for governmental purposes notwithstanding any copyright annotation therein.

References

Walid Ahmad, Elana Simon, Seyone Chithrananda, Gabriel Grand, and Bharath Ramsundar. 2022. Chemberta-2: Towards chemical foundation models. *arXiv preprint arXiv:2209.01712*.

Mugahed Abdullah Hasan Albahde, Bulat Abdrakhimov, Guo-Qi Li, Xiaohu Zhou, Dongkai Zhou, Hao Xu, Huixiao Qian, and Weilin Wang. 2021. The role of microtubules in pancreatic cancer: Therapeutic progress. *Frontiers in Oncology*, 11:640863.

Iz Beltagy, Kyle Lo, and Arman Cohan. 2019. Scibert: A pretrained language model for scientific text. *arXiv preprint arXiv:1903.10676*.

Daniil A Boiko, Robert MacKnight, and Gabe Gomes. 2023. Emergent autonomous scientific research capabilities of large language models. *ArXiv preprint*, abs/2304.05332.

Andres M Bran, Sam Cox, Andrew D White, and Philippe Schwaller. 2023. ChemCrow: Augmenting large-language models with chemistry tools. *arXiv preprint arXiv:2304.05376*.

Cayque Monteiro Castro Nascimento and André Silva Pimentel. 2023. Do large language models understand chemistry? a conversation with chatgpt. *Journal of Chemical Information and Modeling*, 63(6):1649–1655.

Austin H Cheng, Andy Cai, Santiago Miret, Gustavo Malkomes, Mariano Phielipp, and Alán Aspuru-Guzik. 2023. Group selfies: a robust fragment-based molecular string representation. *Digital Discovery*.

Seyone Chithrananda, Gabriel Grand, and Bharath Ramsundar. 2020. Chemberta: Large-scale self-supervised pretraining for molecular property prediction. *arXiv preprint arXiv:2010.09885*.

Dimitrios Christofidellis, Giorgio Giannone, Jannis Born, Ole Winther, Teodoro Laino, and Matteo Manica. 2023. Unifying molecular and textual representations via multi-task language modelling. *arXiv preprint arXiv:2301.12586*.

Carl Edwards, Tuan Lai, Kevin Ros, Garrett Honke, Kyunghyun Cho, and Heng Ji. 2022a. Translation between molecules and natural language. In *Proceedings of the 2022 Conference on Empirical Methods in Natural Language Processing*, pages 375–413, Abu Dhabi, United Arab Emirates. Association for Computational Linguistics.

Carl Edwards, Tuan Lai, Kevin Ros, Garrett Honke, Kyunghyun Cho, and Heng Ji. 2022b. Translation between molecules and natural language. In *Proceedings of the 2022 Conference on Empirical Methods in Natural Language Processing*, pages 375–413, Abu Dhabi, United Arab Emirates. Association for Computational Linguistics.

Carl Edwards, ChengXiang Zhai, and Heng Ji. 2021. Text2Mol: Cross-modal molecule retrieval with natural language queries. In *Proceedings of the 2021 Conference on Empirical Methods in Natural Language Processing*, pages 595–607, Online and Punta Cana, Dominican Republic. Association for Computational Linguistics.

Benedek Fabian, Thomas Edlich, Héléna Gaspar, Marwin Segler, Joshua Meyers, Marco Fiscato, and Mohamed Ahmed. 2020. Molecular representation learning with language models and domain-relevant auxiliary tasks. *arXiv preprint arXiv:2011.13230*.

Yin Fang, Xiaozhuan Liang, Ningyu Zhang, Kangwei Liu, Rui Huang, Zhuo Chen, Xiaohui Fan, and Huajun Chen. 2023. Mol-instructions: A large-scale biomolecular instruction dataset for large language models. *arXiv preprint arXiv:2306.08018*.

Fleur M Ferguson and Nathanael S Gray. 2018. Kinase inhibitors: the road ahead. *Nature reviews Drug discovery*, 17(5):353–377.

Daniel Flam-Shepherd and Alán Aspuru-Guzik. 2023. Language models can generate molecules, materials, and protein binding sites directly in three dimensions as xyz, cif, and pdb files. *arXiv preprint arXiv:2305.05708*.

Nathan Frey, Ryan Soklaski, Simon Axelrod, Siddharth Samsi, Rafael Gómez-Bombarelli, Connor Coley, and Vijay Gadepally. 2022. Neural scaling of deep chemical models.

Miguel García-Ortegón, Gregor N. C. Simm, Austin J. Tripp, José Miguel Hernández-Lobato, Andreas Bender, and Sergio Bacallado. 2022. Dockstring: Easy molecular docking yields better benchmarks for ligand design. *Journal of Chemical Information and Modeling*, 62(15):3486–3502.

Thomas Gaudelet, Ben Day, Arian R Jamasb, Jyothish Soman, Cristian Regep, Gertrude Liu, Jeremy BR Hayter, Richard Vickers, Charles Roberts, Jian Tang, et al. 2021. Utilizing graph machine learning within drug discovery and development. *Briefings in bioinformatics*, 22(6):bbab159.

Francesca Grisoni. 2023. Chemical language models for de novo drug design: Challenges and opportunities. *Current Opinion in Structural Biology*, 79:102527.

Chi Han, Jialiang Xu, Manling Li, Yi R. Fung, Chenkai Sun, Tarek Abdelzaher, and Heng Ji. 2023. Lm-switch: Lightweight language model conditioning in word embedding space. *ArXiv preprint*, abs/2305.12798.

Tom Hope, Doug Downey, Oren Etzioni, and Weld. 2022. A computational inflection for scientific discovery. *ArXiv preprint*, abs/2205.02007.

Allan M Jordan and Stephen D Roughley. 2009. Drug discovery chemistry: a primer for the non-specialist. *Drug discovery today*, 14(15-16):731–744.

Maria Kavallaris. 2010. Microtubules and resistance to tubulin-binding agents. *Nature Reviews Cancer*, 10(3):194–204.

Bernard Kippelen et al. 2009. Organic photovoltaics. *Energy & Environmental Science*, 2(3):251–261.

Mario Krenn, Florian Häse, AkshatKumar Nigam, Pascal Friederich, and Alan Aspuru-Guzik. 2020. Self-referencing embedded strings (selfies): A 100% robust molecular string representation. *Machine Learning: Science and Technology*, 1(4):045024.

Youwei Liang, Ruiyi Zhang, Li Zhang, and Pengtao Xie. 2023. Drugchat: Towards enabling chatgpt-like capabilities on drug molecule graphs.

Shengchao Liu, Weili Nie, Chengpeng Wang, Jiarui Lu, Zhuoran Qiao, Ling Liu, Jian Tang, Chaowei Xiao, and Anima Anandkumar. 2022. Multi-modal molecule structure-text model for text-based retrieval and editing. *arXiv preprint arXiv:2212.10789*.

Shengchao Liu, Jiongxiao Wang, Yijin Yang, Chengpeng Wang, Ling Liu, Hongyu Guo, and Chaowei Xiao. 2023a. Chatgpt-powered conversational drug editing using retrieval and domain feedback. *arXiv preprint arXiv:2305.18090*.

Shengchao Liu, Yutao Zhu, Jiarui Lu, Zhao Xu, Weili Nie, Anthony Gitter, Chaowei Xiao, Jian Tang, Hongyu Guo, and Anima Anandkumar. 2023b. A text-guided protein design framework. *ArXiv preprint*, abs/2302.04611.

Zequn Liu, Wei Zhang, Yingce Xia, Lijun Wu, Shufang Xie, Tao Qin, Ming Zhang, and Tie-Yan Liu. 2023c. Molxpt: Wrapping molecules with text for generative pre-training. *arXiv preprint arXiv:2305.10688*.

Yizhen Luo, Kai Yang, Massimo Hong, Xingyi Liu, and Zaiqing Nie. 2023. Molfm: A multimodal molecular foundation model. *arXiv preprint arXiv:2307.09484*.

Eiman Mukhtar, Vaqar Mustafa Adhami, and Hasan Mukhtar. 2014. Targeting microtubules by natural agents for cancer therapy. *Molecular cancer therapeutics*, 13(2):275–284.

NVIDIA Corporation. 2022. Megamolbart v0.2.

Noel O'Boyle and Andrew Dalke. 2018. Deepsmiles: an adaptation of smiles for use in machine-learning of chemical structures.

Barbara Partee et al. 1984. Compositionality. *Varieties of formal semantics*, 3:281–311.

Philippe Schwaller, Daniel Probst, Alain C Vaucher, Vishnu H Nair, David Kreutter, Teodoro Laino, and Jean-Louis Reymond. 2021. Mapping the space of chemical reactions using attention-based neural networks. *Nature Machine Intelligence*, 3(2):144–152.

Philipp Seidl, Andreu Vall, Sepp Hochreiter, and Günter Klambauer. 2023. Enhancing activity prediction models in drug discovery with the ability to understand human language. *ArXiv preprint*, abs/2303.03363.

Bing Su, Dazhao Du, Zhao Yang, Yujie Zhou, Jiangmeng Li, Anyi Rao, Hao Sun, Zhiwu Lu, and Ji-Rong Wen. 2022. A molecular multimodal foundation model associating molecule graphs with natural language. *ArXiv preprint*, abs/2209.05481.

Zoltán Gendler Szabó. 2020. Compositionality.

Oleg Trott and Arthur J Olson. 2010. Autodock vina: improving the speed and accuracy of docking with a new scoring function, efficient optimization, and multithreading. *Journal of computational chemistry*, 31(2):455–461.

Emma P Tysinger, Brajesh K Rai, and Anton V Sinitskiy. 2023. Can we quickly learn to "translate" bioactive molecules with transformer models? *Journal of Chemical Information and Modeling*, 63(6):1734–1744.

Alain C Vaucher, Philippe Schwaller, Joppe Geluykens, Vishnu H Nair, Anna Iuliano, and Teodoro Laino. 2021. Inferring experimental procedures from text-based representations of chemical reactions. *Nature communications*, 12(1):2573.

Alain C Vaucher, Federico Zipoli, Joppe Geluykens, Vishnu H Nair, Philippe Schwaller, and Teodoro Laino. 2020. Automated extraction of chemical synthesis actions from experimental procedures. *Nature communications*, 11(1):3601.

Hanchen Wang, Tianfan Fu, Yuanqi Du, Wenhao Gao, Kexin Huang, Ziming Liu, Payal Chandak, Shengchao Liu, Peter Van Katwyk, Andreea Deac, et al. 2023. Scientific discovery in the age of artificial intelligence. *Nature*, 620(7972):47–60.

Onsurang Wattanathamsan and Varisa Pongrakhananon. 2022. Emerging role of microtubule-associated proteins on cancer metastasis. *Frontiers in Pharmacology*, 13:935493.

Jason Wei, Maarten Bosma, Vincent Y Zhao, Kelvin Guu, Adams Wei Yu, Brian Lester, Nan Du, Andrew M Dai, and Quoc V Le. 2021. Finetuned language models are zero-shot learners. *arXiv preprint arXiv:2109.01652*.

David Weininger. 1988. Smiles, a chemical language and information system. 1. introduction to methodology and encoding rules. *Journal of Chemical Information and Computer Sciences*, 28(1):31–36.

Andrew D White, Glen M Hocky, Heta A Gandhi, Mehrad Ansari, Sam Cox, Geemi P Wellawatte, Subarna Sasmal, Ziyue Yang, Kangxin Liu, Yuvraj Singh, et al. 2023. Assessment of chemistry knowledge in large language models that generate code. *Digital Discovery*, 2(2):368–376.

Hanwen Xu, Addie Woicik, Hoifung Poon, Russ B Altman, and Sheng Wang. 2023. Multilingual translation for zero-shot biomedical classification using biotranslator. *Nature Communications*, 14(1):738.

Zheni Zeng, Yuan Yao, Zhiyuan Liu, and Maosong Sun. 2022. A deep-learning system bridging molecule structure and biomedical text with comprehension comparable to human professionals. *Nature communications*, 13(1):862.

Zheni Zeng, Bangchen Yin, Shipeng Wang, Jiarui Liu, Cheng Yang, Haishen Yao, Xingzhi Sun, Maosong Sun, Guotong Xie, and Zhiyuan Liu. 2023. Interactive molecular discovery with natural language. *arXiv preprint arXiv:2306.11976*.

Xuan Zhang, Limei Wang, Jacob Helwig, Youzhi Luo, Cong Fu, Yaochen Xie, Meng Liu, Yuchao Lin, Zhao Xu, Keqiang Yan, et al. 2023. Artificial intelligence for science in quantum, atomistic, and continuum systems. *arXiv preprint arXiv:2307.08423*.

Haiteng Zhao, Shengchao Liu, Chang Ma, Hannan Xu, Jie Fu, Zhi-Hong Deng, Lingpeng Kong, and Qi Liu. 2023a. Gimlet: A unified graph-text model for instruction-based molecule zero-shot learning. *bioRxiv*, pages 2023–05.

Wenyu Zhao, Dong Zhou, Buqing Cao, Kai Zhang, and Jinjun Chen. 2023b. Adversarial modality alignment network for cross-modal molecule retrieval. *IEEE Transactions on Artificial Intelligence*.

C Lawrence Zitnick, Lowik Chanussot, Abhishek Das, Siddharth Goyal, Javier Heras-Domingo, Caleb Ho, Weihua Hu, Thibaut Lavril, Aini Palizhati, Morgane Riviere, et al. 2020. An introduction to electrocatalyst design using machine learning for renewable energy storage. *arXiv preprint arXiv:2010.09435*.

Transformer-specific Interpretability

Hosein Mohebbi[1] **Jaap Jumelet**[2] **Michael Hanna**[2] **Afra Alishahi**[1] **Willem Zuidema**[2]
[1] Tilburg University [2] University of Amsterdam
{h.mohebbi, a.alishahi}@tilburguniversity.edu
{j.w.d.jumelet, m.w.hanna, w.h.zuidema}@uva.nl

Abstract

Transformers have emerged as dominant players in various scientific fields, especially NLP. However, their inner workings, like many other neural networks, remain opaque. In spite of the widespread use of model-agnostic interpretability techniques, including gradient-based and occlusion-based, their shortcomings are becoming increasingly apparent for Transformer interpretation, making the field of interpretability more demanding today. In this tutorial, we will present Transformer-specific interpretability methods, a new trending approach, that make use of specific features of the Transformer architecture and are deemed more promising for understanding Transformer-based models. We start by discussing the potential pitfalls and misleading results model-agnostic approaches may produce when interpreting Transformers. Next, we discuss Transformer-specific methods, including those designed to quantify context-mixing interactions among all input pairs (as the fundamental property of the Transformer architecture) and those that combine causal methods with low-level Transformer analysis to identify particular subnetworks within a model that are responsible for specific tasks. By the end of the tutorial, we hope participants will understand the advantages (as well as current limitations) of Transformer-specific interpretability methods, along with how these can be applied to their own research.

1 Tutorial Description

With Transformers (Vaswani et al., 2017) demonstrating exceptional performance across every domain they venture into such as language, speech, vision, and music, the necessity to understand their underlying mechanisms has become more crucial than ever before. Many model-agnostic interpretability techniques that were commonly used for earlier generations of deep learning architectures, such as probing, occlusion-based, and feature attribution methods, were swiftly adapted for use with the Transformer architecture. However, these approaches demonstrate notable disagreement with each other and a lack of stability when moving from one domain to another (Neely et al., 2022; Pruthi et al., 2020; Krishna et al., 2022). Their effectiveness in drawing reliable conclusions has therefore been an ongoing matter of debate (Bibal et al., 2022).

Recently, a game-changing trend has emerged: the development of analysis methods that are precisely tailored to the model architecture of Transformers, built upon their underlying mathematical foundations. These methods make use of specific features of Transformers, including their layered structure (layers, heads, tokens), the division of labor between the attention mechanism, feed-forward layers, and residual streams. These techniques span from those aimed at measuring token-to-token interactions (known as *context mixing*, Brunner et al., 2020; Kobayashi et al., 2020, 2021; Ferrando et al., 2022b; Mohebbi et al., 2023b,a), to others striving to reverse engineer the model decision and decompose it into understandable pieces (known as *mechanistic interpretability*, Wang et al., 2023; Elhage et al., 2021).

This tutorial focuses on Transformer-specific interpretability methods. We will first briefly review the internal structure of the Transformer architecture to establish our notations. Next, we will explain why it is necessary to design methods tailored to the model architecture, exposing the limitations of model-agnostic approaches when applied to Transformer analysis using practical examples. Subsequently, we will introduce Transformer-specific techniques, delving into their mathematics, and categorizing them according to their purposes, using experimental results across a number of domains, such as text, speech, and music, as well as across several languages. Our tutorial will conclude with a discussion on current limitations in interpretability and promising future directions.

Proceedings of the 18th Conference of the European Chapter of the Association for Computational Linguistics Tutorial Abstracts, pages 21–26
March 21, 2024

2 Tutorial Type

The tutorial will be cutting-edge, covering the latest research advancements in the interpretability of Transformers, which serve as the backbone architecture of modern NLP systems.

The only ACL tutorials similar to ours are "Interpretability and Analysis in Neural NLP" (Belinkov et al., 2020) and "Fine-grained Interpretation and Causation Analysis in Deep NLP Models" (Sajjad et al., 2021), held at ACL 2020 and NAACL 2021, respectively. Both focused on general model-agnostic interpretability techniques. Our tutorial, however, will question the effectiveness of those general-purpose analysis methods and mark the next chapter: a transition from model-agnostic approaches to Transformer-specific methods.

3 Target Audience

Given the widespread use of Transformers across various applications in both text and speech, we expect that our audience will be not only folks engaged in interpretability but also those from various tracks within the Computational Linguistics community who have not kept up with the recent advancements within interpretability research. In fact, we have been frequently asked at *ACL conferences and our industry meetings, particularly by individuals outside of the interpretability track, seeking guidance on the most effective interpretability techniques to employ in their projects for non-interpretability purposes, such as training monitoring, model compression, or model tuning.

In terms of expected prerequisite background, we expect audience members to be familiar with the basic concepts of Transformer models. For the Jupyter notebooks that will be covered, we expect experience with PyTorch and the `Transformers` library.

4 Outline of Tutorial Structure

The tutorial will consist of 30 minute slots of lectures and interactive seminars for which we will provide Jupyter notebooks. A small part of the tutorial will be focused on interpretability techniques from the organisers (e.g. Abnar and Zuidema, 2020 and Mohebbi et al., 2023b), but the majority of the work discussed will be work from other labs to provide an honest and broad overview of the current state of interpretability research in NLP.

1. 30 minute lecture on **model-agnostic interpretability**:
   - Introduction
   - Model-agnostic approaches: probing, feature attributions, behavioral studies
   - How are model-agnostic approaches adapted to Transformers? What are their limitations?

2. 30 minute lecture on interpretation of **attention** and **context mixing**:
   - Attention analysis (Clark et al., 2019) as a straightforward starting point for measuring context mixing.
   - Limitations of interpreting raw attention scores (Bibal et al., 2022; Hassid et al., 2022)
   - Effective attention scores: rollout (Abnar and Zuidema, 2020), HTA (Brunner et al., 2020), LRP-based attention (Chefer et al., 2020).
   - Expanding the scope of context mixing analysis by incorporating other model components: Attention-Norm (Kobayashi et al., 2020, 2021, 2023), GlobEnc (Modarressi et al., 2022), ALTI (Ferrando et al., 2022b,a), Value Zeroing (Mohebbi et al., 2023b), DecompX (Modarressi et al., 2023).

3. 30 minute interactive tutorial on interpreting context mixing: Jupyter notebooks will be provided (via Google Colab) and can be run interactively while the presenters go through it.

4. Coffee break

5. 30 minute lecture on **mechanistic** and **causality-based** interpretability:
   - Basics of mechanistic interpretability: the residual stream and computational graph views of models, and the circuits framework (Olah et al., 2020; Elhage et al., 2021; Hanna et al., 2023).
   - Finding circuit structure using causal interventions (Vig et al., 2020; Geiger et al., 2021; Wang et al., 2023; Goldowsky-Dill et al., 2023; Conmy et al., 2023; Nanda, 2023; Syed et al., 2023).

- Assigning semantics to circuit components: the logit lens (Nostalgebrist, 2020; Geva et al., 2021), concept erasure (Belrose et al., 2023), and (potentially) polysemanticity and superposition (Elhage et al., 2022).

6. 30 minute interactive tutorial mechanistic interpretability in NLP, notebooks will again be provided.

7. 30 minute slot for discussion, reflection and future outlook: what are open questions in interpretability, what's next, and what's lacking?

5 Reading List

In addition to the key papers mentioned in Section 4, we would recommend attendees that are interested in gaining a broader understanding of general interpretability techniques to explore the following survey papers: (Belinkov and Glass, 2019; Madsen et al., 2021; Raukur et al., 2022; Lyu et al., 2022)

6 Special Requirements

There are no special technical requirements, other than standard conference equipment (computer, screen, and projector). If participants wish to participate in the interactive parts, they should bring their laptops.

7 Diversity

Our tutorial focuses on Transformer-specific interpretability across several domains, including text, speech, music, (and vision, to some extent). As Transformers have gained widespread adoption within the CL community, we anticipate engaging a diverse and extensive audience. To ensure diversity, we have both professors and PhD students on our instructor team.

8 Tutorial Instructors

Hosein Mohebbi is a PhD candidate at Tilburg University. He is part of the InDeep consortium project, doing research on the interpretability of deep neural models for both text and speech. During his Master's, his research revolved around the interpretation of pre-trained language models and the utilization of interpretability techniques to accelerate their inference time. His research has been published in leading NLP venues such as ACL, EACL, EMNLP, and BlackboxNLP, where he also regularly serves as a reviewer. He is also one of the organizers of BlackboxNLP 2023-2024, a workshop focusing on analyzing and interpreting neural networks for NLP.

Jaap Jumelet is a PhD candidate at the Institute for Logic, Language and Computation at the University of Amsterdam. His research focuses on gaining an understanding of how neural models are able to build up hierarchical representations of their input, by leveraging hypotheses from (psycho-)linguistics. His research has been published at leading NLP venues, including TACL, ACL, and CoNLL. He is a co-organiser for BlackboxNLP in 2023-2024. He has been involved in numerous courses in the AI Master of the University of Amsterdam, all with a focus on NLP and interpretability.

Michael Hanna is a PhD candidate at the University of Amsterdam, as part of the Institute for Logic, Language and Computation. His research focuses on understanding the abilities of pre-trained language models, and linking these behaviors to low-level mechanisms using causal methods. His work has been published in leading interpretability and NLP venues such as NeurIPS, EMNLP, and EACL. He previously designed and led a workshop on mechanistic interpretability as part of the University of Amsterdam's artificial intelligence masters program.

Afra Alishahi is an Associate Professor at the Department of Cognitive Science and Artificial Intelligence at Tilburg University, Netherlands. Her main research interests are developing computational models of human language, studying the emergence of linguistic structure in grounded models of language learning, and developing tools and techniques for analyzing linguistic representations in neural models of language. She has served as program chair for CoNLL and as AC and SAC for many recent CL conferences, and is one of the founders of the BlackboxNLP workshops. She has acted as ACL tutorial co-chair and taught tutorials at ACL and ESSLII; most recently she offered a tutorial on *Interpretability of linguistic knowledge in neural language models* as part of Lectures on Computational Linguistics in Pisa, Italy.

Willem Zuidema is Associate Professor of NLP, Explainable AI and Cognitive Modelling at the University of Amsterdam. He has published widely in NLP, AI and Cognitive Science venues, including TACL, JAIR, ACL, EMNLP and NeurIPS. Since 2016, many of his publications have focused on interpretability in AI. He has taught many undergraduate and graduate courses (including Interpretability and Explainability in AI in Amsterdams's MSc AI, 2022, 2023), and two courses at graduate summerschools (ESSLLI 2008, 2015). He leads a project on interpretability that involves 5 universities ('InDeep', 2021-2026). He has served on many program committees, including ACL, NAACL, EMNLP, BlackboxNLP, and helped organize workshops and conferences; in 2016, he was tutorial co-chair for ACL.

References

Samira Abnar and Willem Zuidema. 2020. Quantifying attention flow in transformers. In *Proceedings of the 58th Annual Meeting of the Association for Computational Linguistics*, pages 4190–4197, Online. Association for Computational Linguistics.

Yonatan Belinkov, Sebastian Gehrmann, and Ellie Pavlick. 2020. Interpretability and analysis in neural NLP. In *Proceedings of the 58th Annual Meeting of the Association for Computational Linguistics: Tutorial Abstracts*, pages 1–5, Online. Association for Computational Linguistics.

Yonatan Belinkov and James Glass. 2019. Analysis methods in neural language processing: A survey. *Transactions of the Association for Computational Linguistics*, 7:49–72.

Nora Belrose, David Schneider-Joseph, Shauli Ravfogel, Ryan Cotterell, Edward Raff, and Stella Biderman. 2023. Leace: Perfect linear concept erasure in closed form.

Adrien Bibal, Rémi Cardon, David Alfter, Rodrigo Wilkens, Xiaoou Wang, Thomas François, and Patrick Watrin. 2022. Is attention explanation? an introduction to the debate. In *Proceedings of the 60th Annual Meeting of the Association for Computational Linguistics (Volume 1: Long Papers)*, pages 3889–3900, Dublin, Ireland. Association for Computational Linguistics.

Gino Brunner, Yang Liu, Damian Pascual, Oliver Richter, Massimiliano Ciaramita, and Roger Wattenhofer. 2020. On identifiability in transformers. In *International Conference on Learning Representations*.

Hila Chefer, Shir Gur, and Lior Wolf. 2020. Transformer interpretability beyond attention visualization. *2021 IEEE/CVF Conference on Computer Vision and Pattern Recognition (CVPR)*, pages 782–791.

Kevin Clark, Urvashi Khandelwal, Omer Levy, and Christopher D. Manning. 2019. What does BERT look at? an analysis of BERT's attention. In *Proceedings of the 2019 ACL Workshop BlackboxNLP: Analyzing and Interpreting Neural Networks for NLP*, pages 276–286, Florence, Italy. Association for Computational Linguistics.

Arthur Conmy, Augustine N. Mavor-Parker, Aengus Lynch, Stefan Heimersheim, and Adrià Garriga-Alonso. 2023. Towards automated circuit discovery for mechanistic interpretability.

Nelson Elhage, Tristan Hume, Catherine Olsson, Nicholas Schiefer, Tom Henighan, Shauna Kravec, Zac Hatfield-Dodds, Robert Lasenby, Dawn Drain, Carol Chen, Roger Grosse, Sam McCandlish, Jared Kaplan, Dario Amodei, Martin Wattenberg, and Christopher Olah. 2022. Toy models of superposition. *Transformer Circuits Thread*.

Nelson Elhage, Neel Nanda, Catherine Olsson, Tom Henighan, Nicholas Joseph, Ben Mann, Amanda Askell, Yuntao Bai, Anna Chen, Tom Conerly, Nova DasSarma, Dawn Drain, Deep Ganguli, Zac Hatfield-Dodds, Danny Hernandez, Andy Jones, Jackson Kernion, Liane Lovitt, Kamal Ndousse, Dario Amodei, Tom Brown, Jack Clark, Jared Kaplan, Sam McCandlish, and Chris Olah. 2021. A mathematical framework for transformer circuits. *Transformer Circuits Thread*. Https://transformer-circuits.pub/2021/framework/index.html.

Javier Ferrando, Gerard I. Gállego, Belen Alastruey, Carlos Escolano, and Marta R. Costa-jussà. 2022a. Towards opening the black box of neural machine translation: Source and target interpretations of the transformer. In *Proceedings of the 2022 Conference on Empirical Methods in Natural Language Processing*, pages 8756–8769, Abu Dhabi, United Arab Emirates. Association for Computational Linguistics.

Javier Ferrando, Gerard I. Gállego, and Marta R. Costa-jussà. 2022b. Measuring the mixing of contextual information in the transformer. In *Proceedings of the 2022 Conference on Empirical Methods in Natural Language Processing*, pages 8698–8714, Abu Dhabi, United Arab Emirates. Association for Computational Linguistics.

Atticus Geiger, Hanson Lu, Thomas Icard, and Christopher Potts. 2021. Causal abstractions of neural networks. In *Advances in Neural Information Processing Systems 34: Annual Conference on Neural Information Processing Systems 2021, NeurIPS 2021, December 6-14, 2021, virtual*, pages 9574–9586.

Mor Geva, Roei Schuster, Jonathan Berant, and Omer Levy. 2021. Transformer feed-forward layers are key-value memories. In *Proceedings of the 2021 Conference on Empirical Methods in Natural Language Processing*, pages 5484–5495, Online and Punta Cana,

Dominican Republic. Association for Computational Linguistics.

Nicholas Goldowsky-Dill, Chris MacLeod, Lucas Sato, and Aryaman Arora. 2023. Localizing model behavior with path patching.

Michael Hanna, Ollie Liu, and Alexandre Variengien. 2023. How does GPT-2 compute greater-than?: Interpreting mathematical abilities in a pre-trained language model. In *Thirty-seventh Conference on Neural Information Processing Systems*.

Michael Hassid, Hao Peng, Daniel Rotem, Jungo Kasai, Ivan Montero, Noah A. Smith, and Roy Schwartz. 2022. How much does attention actually attend? questioning the importance of attention in pretrained transformers. In *Findings of the Association for Computational Linguistics: EMNLP 2022*, pages 1403–1416, Abu Dhabi, United Arab Emirates. Association for Computational Linguistics.

Goro Kobayashi, Tatsuki Kuribayashi, Sho Yokoi, and Kentaro Inui. 2020. Attention is not only a weight: Analyzing transformers with vector norms. In *Proceedings of the 2020 Conference on Empirical Methods in Natural Language Processing (EMNLP)*, pages 7057–7075, Online. Association for Computational Linguistics.

Goro Kobayashi, Tatsuki Kuribayashi, Sho Yokoi, and Kentaro Inui. 2021. Incorporating Residual and Normalization Layers into Analysis of Masked Language Models. In *Proceedings of the 2021 Conference on Empirical Methods in Natural Language Processing*, pages 4547–4568, Online and Punta Cana, Dominican Republic. Association for Computational Linguistics.

Goro Kobayashi, Tatsuki Kuribayashi, Sho Yokoi, and Kentaro Inui. 2023. Feed-forward blocks control contextualization in masked language models. *ArXiv*, abs/2302.00456.

Satyapriya Krishna, Tessa Han, Alex Gu, Javin Pombra, Shahin Jabbari, Steven Wu, and Himabindu Lakkaraju. 2022. The disagreement problem in explainable machine learning: A practitioner's perspective. *ArXiv*, abs/2202.01602.

Qing Lyu, Marianna Apidianaki, and Chris Callison-Burch. 2022. Towards faithful model explanation in nlp: A survey. *ArXiv*, abs/2209.11326.

Andreas Madsen, Siva Reddy, and A. P. Sarath Chandar. 2021. Post-hoc interpretability for neural nlp: A survey. *ACM Computing Surveys*, 55:1 – 42.

Ali Modarressi, Mohsen Fayyaz, Ehsan Aghazadeh, Yadollah Yaghoobzadeh, and Mohammad Taher Pilehvar. 2023. DecompX: Explaining transformers decisions by propagating token decomposition. In *Proceedings of the 61st Annual Meeting of the Association for Computational Linguistics (Volume 1: Long Papers)*, pages 2649–2664, Toronto, Canada. Association for Computational Linguistics.

Ali Modarressi, Mohsen Fayyaz, Yadollah Yaghoobzadeh, and Mohammad Taher Pilehvar. 2022. GlobEnc: Quantifying global token attribution by incorporating the whole encoder layer in transformers. In *Proceedings of the 2022 Conference of the North American Chapter of the Association for Computational Linguistics: Human Language Technologies*, pages 258–271, Seattle, United States. Association for Computational Linguistics.

Hosein Mohebbi, Grzegorz Chrupała, Willem Zuidema, and Afra Alishahi. 2023a. Homophone disambiguation reveals patterns of context mixing in speech transformers. In *Proceedings of the 2023 Conference on Empirical Methods in Natural Language Processing*, pages 8249–8260, Singapore. Association for Computational Linguistics.

Hosein Mohebbi, Willem Zuidema, Grzegorz Chrupała, and Afra Alishahi. 2023b. Quantifying context mixing in transformers. In *Proceedings of the 17th Conference of the European Chapter of the Association for Computational Linguistics*, pages 3378–3400, Dubrovnik, Croatia. Association for Computational Linguistics.

Neel Nanda. 2023. Attribution patching: Activation patching at industrial scale.

Michael Neely, Stefan F. Schouten, Maurits J. R. Bleeker, and Ana Lucic. 2022. A song of (dis)agreement: Evaluating the evaluation of explainable artificial intelligence in natural language processing. In *HHAI*.

Nostalgebrist. 2020. interpreting GPT: the logit lens.

Chris Olah, Nick Cammarata, Ludwig Schubert, Gabriel Goh, Michael Petrov, and Shan Carter. 2020. Zoom in: An introduction to circuits. *Distill*. Https://distill.pub/2020/circuits/zoom-in.

Danish Pruthi, Bhuwan Dhingra, Livio Baldini Soares, Michael Collins, Zachary Chase Lipton, Graham Neubig, and William W. Cohen. 2020. Evaluating explanations: How much do explanations from the teacher aid students? *Transactions of the Association for Computational Linguistics*, 10:359–375.

Tilman Raukur, An Chang Ho, Stephen Casper, and Dylan Hadfield-Menell. 2022. Toward transparent ai: A survey on interpreting the inner structures of deep neural networks. *2023 IEEE Conference on Secure and Trustworthy Machine Learning (SaTML)*, pages 464–483.

Hassan Sajjad, Narine Kokhlikyan, Fahim Dalvi, and Nadir Durrani. 2021. Fine-grained interpretation and causation analysis in deep NLP models. In *Proceedings of the 2021 Conference of the North American Chapter of the Association for Computational Linguistics: Human Language Technologies: Tutorials*, pages 5–10, Online. Association for Computational Linguistics.

Aaquib Syed, Can Rager, and Arthur Conmy. 2023. Attribution patching outperforms automated circuit discovery.

Ashish Vaswani, Noam Shazeer, Niki Parmar, Jakob Uszkoreit, Llion Jones, Aidan N Gomez, Łukasz Kaiser, and Illia Polosukhin. 2017. Attention is all you need. *Advances in neural information processing systems*, 30.

Jesse Vig, Sebastian Gehrmann, Yonatan Belinkov, Sharon Qian, Daniel Nevo, Yaron Singer, and Stuart M. Shieber. 2020. Investigating gender bias in language models using causal mediation analysis. In *Advances in Neural Information Processing Systems 33: Annual Conference on Neural Information Processing Systems 2020, NeurIPS 2020, December 6-12, 2020, virtual*.

Kevin Ro Wang, Alexandre Variengien, Arthur Conmy, Buck Shlegeris, and Jacob Steinhardt. 2023. Interpretability in the wild: a circuit for indirect object identification in GPT-2 small. In *The Eleventh International Conference on Learning Representations*.

LLMs for Low Resource Languages in Multilingual, Multimodal and Dialectal Settings

Firoj Alam, Shammur Absar Chowdhury, Sabri Boughorbel, Maram Hasanain
Qatar Computing Research Institute, HBKU, Doha, Qatar
{fialam, shchowdhury, sboughorbel, mhasanain}@hbku.edu.qa

Abstract

The recent breakthroughs in Artificial Intelligence (AI) can be attributed to the remarkable performance of Large Language Models (LLMs) across a spectrum of research areas (e.g., machine translation, question-answering, automatic speech recognition, text-to-speech generation) and application domains (e.g., business, law, healthcare, education, and psychology). The success of these LLMs largely depends on specific training techniques, most notably instruction tuning, RLHF, and subsequent prompting to achieve the desired output. As the development of such LLMs continues to increase in both closed and open settings, evaluation has become crucial for understanding their generalization capabilities across different tasks, modalities, languages, and dialects. This evaluation process is tightly coupled with prompting, which plays a key role in obtaining better outputs. There has been attempts to evaluate such models focusing on diverse tasks, languages, and dialects, which suggests that the capabilities of LLMs are still limited to medium-to-low-resource languages due to the lack of representative datasets. The tutorial offers an overview of this emerging research area. We explore the capabilities of LLMs in terms of their performance, zero- and few-shot settings, fine-tuning, instructions tuning, and close vs. open models with a special emphasis on low-resource settings. In addition to LLMs for standard NLP tasks, we will focus on speech and multimodality.[1]

1 Tutorial Content Description

Large Language Models (LLMs) are prominent examples of Foundation Models (FMs), based on the Transformer network architecture (Vaswani et al., 2017). Trained to predict the subsequent token in a sequence, LLMs capture implicit and intricate information contained in the data. Moreover, when created using multilingual training data, the models capture linguistic nuances, phonological patterns, and semantic relationships across languages, strengthening its multilingual capabilities. However, understanding how their capabilities generalize across tasks and languages requires a systematic evaluation approach.

1.1 Benchmarking LLMs for different tasks and languages

The HELM project (Liang et al., 2022) assessed English LLMs across various metrics and scenarios. BIG-Bench (Srivastava et al., 2022) introduced a large-scale evaluation with 214 tasks, considering low-resource languages as well. Other efforts included evaluations of ChatGPT, GPT2.5, BLOOMZ, and OpenAI GPT as in Bang et al. (2023); Ahuja et al. (2023); Hendy et al. (2023); Abdelali et al. (2023); Scao et al. (2022).

For speech, OpenAI's Whisper (Radford et al., 2022), Google's USM (Zhang et al., 2023), and other speech models are explored by the speech community. They are general-purpose speech models with multilingual capabilities, designed for speech recognition (ASR) and other tasks. The benchmarking efforts include Speech Processing Universal PERformance Benchmark (SUPERB) initiative (Yang et al., 2021) which includes a collection of benchmarking tools, resources, and a leader board for 10 tasks from six domains.

1.2 LLMs and lower-resources languages

These LLMs have been trained on datasets from the internet, ingesting many resources in different languages. For close models (e.g., ChatGPT) the coverage and the distribution of the content for medium-to-low-resource languages are unknown. Most of the open-sourced models uses common-crawl dataset, which is skewed for many languages. For example, Bloom, that is trained on 46 natural

[1]The content of the tutorial will be available at the following website: `https://llm-low-resource-lang.github.io/`.

Proceedings of the 18th Conference of the European Chapter of the Association for Computational Linguistics
Tutorial Abstracts, pages 27–33
March 21, 2024

languages and 13 programming languages [2], has only 4.6%, 0.02% and 0.70% language coverage for Arabic, Swahili and Hindi respectively (Scao et al., 2022).

With models trained on such distribution of data, this raises questions on their capabilities on medium-to-low-resource languages in a variety of language processing tasks. To understand the capabilities of LLMs, there has been several research efforts. Bang et al. (2023) reports that ChatGPT fails to generalize to low and extremely low resources languages (e.g., Marathi, Sundanese, and Buginese). Lai et al. (2023) reports that ChatGPT generally performs better for English than other languages. Ahuja et al. (2023) evaluate 8 different tasks with 33 languages and report that LLMs perform better on high-resource languages and languages that are in Latin scripts. In our work for Arabic, we evaluate ChatGPT on 33 tasks, 59 datasets with 96 test setups using zero-shot setting. Performances are significantly lower on 88 test setups (Abdelali et al., 2023). This study also focused on tasks covering different Arabic dialects and reports that models perform comparably for MSA than other dialects such as Egyptian, Gulf, Levantine, and Maghrebi.

In the realm of speech technology, OpenAI's recent Whisper model has demonstrated that the performance in low-resource languages is still relatively poor, a trend that correlates with the size of the pre-training dataset. Subsequently, Google's USM models have shown further improvements in performance, achieving an average word error rate (WER) of less than 30% across 73 languages.

1.3 Multimodality

Along side with NLP, speech, and multimodal generative models have also emerged (Liu et al., 2023a; Zhu et al., 2023a; OpenAI, 2023a). ChatGPT has demonstrated multi-modal abilities on variety of tasks. Following that, Zhu et al. (2023a) developed MiniGPT-4, which is trained by combining Vicuna (Chiang et al., 2023) and Blip-2 (Li et al., 2023). Recently, OpenAI, Google, and Meta released GPT-4 Vision (OpenAI, 2023b), Gemini (Team et al., 2023), and AnyMAL (Moon et al., 2023), respectively, each focusing on multimodal aspects. The idea of the these attempts was to train a model by aligning visual information from a pre-trained vision encoder with an LLM. Though their capabilities have not been widely studied across tasks and languages, it is important to explore and understand their capabilities that can enhance future studies.

[2] https://huggingface.co/bigscience/bloom

1.4 Dialects

In our study for Arabic (Abdelali et al., 2023), we observed that the gaps in LLMs' performance between MSA and dialectal datasets (e.g., for machine translation (MT) and speech recognition task) are more pronounced, indicating ineffectiveness of LLMs for under-represented dialects. For example, in both the GPT-models, we noticed a large discrepancy in the POS accuracy of 0.810 versus 0.379 on MSA and dialects respectively. Similarly, for Arabic dialect identification tasks (ADI) we notice a significant difference between the SOTA acoustic and lexical model with respect to LLMs results.

1.5 Prompting for LLMs

Prompt design plays a critical role in influencing the performance of Large Language Models (LLMs), as evidenced in (Reynolds and McDonell, 2021; Dong et al., 2022). These models are highly sensitive to minor variations in the prompts, such as word choice and the order of examples in few-shot settings. Ahuja et al. (2023) have investigated various monolingual and multilingual prompts, discovering that English-language templates generally outperform those in native languages. The performance of a task also depends on native and non-native language prompts. In our study focusing on Arabic (Abdelali et al., 2023) and Bangla (Hasan et al., 2023), we have found that performance can vary considerably depending on whether the prompts are in a native or non-native language. This variability is observed in both zero-shot and few-shot settings. Another point of interest in few-shot settings is the method used for selecting shots and arranging them in a reasonable order. Various approaches have been reported, such as random selection (Khondaker et al., 2023), class-based selection (e.g., Liang et al. (2022) selected examples to ensure class coverage in classification tasks), and Maximal Marginal Relevance-based (MMR) selection (Carbonell and Goldstein, 1998).

1.6 What this tutorial offers

Here, we provide an overview of the capabilities of LLMs for diverse tasks, languages, dialects, and modalities, including text, speech, and multimodality. We start with an introduction to LLMs, including a brief history and their significant capabilities in downstream tasks. This is followed by an in-depth examination of various LLMs developed for NLP, speech, and multimodal applications, emphasizing their utility across different tasks.

In the third part of the tutorial, we delve into the intricacies of prompting, which serves as a foundational element for obtaining output from these LLMs. In this part, we will also include a hands-on demonstration of tools that have been developed to further facilitate research on LLMs. The fourth part of the tutorial will focus on a more comprehensive discussion about low-resource languages, addressing both the challenges they present and future directions for research. Finally, we will discuss hallucination, bias, toxicity, and computational resources needed for model training and inference. An outline of the tutorial is reported in Section 3.

2 Type of the Tutorial

The tutorial is both introductory, covering a number of topics related to the capabilities of LLMs, but it is also cutting-edge, covering some latest developments in these areas. Attendees will have an overview of tasks, languages, dialects and modalities related to LLMs, which will put them up to speed to do research in the area. The tutorial targets anyone interested in employing LLMs for NLP, speech and multimodal tasks. We believe researchers working on lower-resource languages will be especially interested. We expect the audience to have intermediate machine learning knowledge.

3 Outline of the Tutorial

Below, we offer an outline of the tutorial. More information and materials will is available online on the tutorial website upon the tutorial acceptance.

3.1 Introduction [30 min]

(i) LLMs
- (a) A brief history of LLMs
- (b) Capabilities in downstream NLP, speech, and multimodal tasks

References: (Mielke et al., 2021; Sennrich et al., 2016; Wu et al., 2016; Kudo and Richardson, 2018; Radford et al., 2019; Devlin et al., 2019; Liu et al., 2019; Lewis et al., 2020)

3.2 Models and their capabilities for low-resource languages [30 min]

The following are just a few examples of models. They will not be the only ones covered in the tutorial.

(i) Models for NLP tasks
- (a) GPT 3.5 (ChatGPT), GPT-4
- (b) Bloom, LLaMA, mT5, Flan, PaLM

(ii) Models for Speech tasks
- (a) USM
- (b) Whisper

(iii) Models for Multimodality
- (a) Closed models: GPT-4 Vision, Gemini
- (b) Open Models: MiniGPT, LLaVA

References: (Brown et al., 2020; Liu et al., 2023a; Xue et al., 2020; Scao et al., 2022; Touvron et al., 2023; Zhu et al., 2023a)

3.3 Prompt Engineering [50 min]

(i) Zero-shot

(ii) Few-shots and selection methods

(iii) Prompt templates

(iv) Mono/Cross lingual prompting

(v) Prompt programming

(vi) Tools and resources (e.g., LLMeBench (Dalvi et al., 2023), OpenICL (Wu et al., 2023), PromptBench (Zhu et al., 2023b)) and lm-evaluation-harness (Gao et al., 2023).

References: (Wei et al., 2021; Zhang et al., 2022; Reynolds and McDonell, 2021)

3.4 Limitations and Challenges for low-resource settings [50 min]

(i) Multitask, multilingual, multimodal evaluation for low-resource languages

(ii) Multi-dialects challenges

(iii) Summary of recent benchmarking efforts

References: (Ahuja et al., 2023; Liang et al., 2022; Srivastava et al., 2022; Bang et al., 2023; Ahuja et al., 2023; Hendy et al., 2023; Yang et al., 2021; Radford et al., 2022; Zhang et al., 2023; Abdelali et al., 2023; Bang et al., 2023; Bubeck et al., 2023)

3.5 Other Related Aspects [30 min]

(i) Hallucination

(ii) Bias, Toxicity and Misinformation in LLMs

(iii) Computational Resources, Carbon footprint

References: (Bang et al., 2023)

4 Prerequisites

We expect attendees to be equipped with basic knowledge of machine learning, including familiarity with recent neural network architectures, particularly Transformers, and an understanding of pre-trained language models. Additionally, attendees should be familiar with standard NLP tasks such as text classification, natural language generation, and question answering.

5 Reading List

In addition to the references cited in Section 3, we recommend several surveys: an overview of LLMs (Zhao et al., 2023), prompt engineering (Liu et al., 2023b; Gu et al., 2023), in-context learning (Dong et al., 2022), and evaluation of LLMs (Liang et al., 2022).

6 Tutorial Instructors

Firoj Alam is a Scientist at the Qatar Computing Research Institute (QCRI), HBKU. He received his PhD from the University of Trento, Italy, and has been working for more than ten years in Artificial Intelligence, Deep/machine learning, Natural Language Processing, Social media content, Image Processing, and Conversation Analysis. His current research interest includes LLMs, fact-checking, multimodal propaganda detection in multiple languages. He previously presented tutorials at WWW-2022 and WSDM-2022 on the topic of "Fact-Checking, Fake News, Propaganda, And Media Bias". He was a co-organizer of different shared tasks CheckThat! 2020-2024 at CLEF, SemEval-2021 task 6 (propaganda detection in memes), SemEval-2024 task (multilingual detection of persuasion techniques in memes), WANLP (Arabic-NLP) shared task (2022-2023) and the NLP4IF-2021 shared task. He is also a co-organizer of the BLP-2023 workshop (collocated with EMNLP-2023).

Shammur Absar Chowdhury is a Scientist at QCRI, HBKU. Her research interest includes designing speech models, and interpretability for atypical phenomena in conversation. Dr. Chowdhury authored more than 60 peer-reviewed publications in tier-top conferences and journals; and actively contributed to the research community by organizing shared tasks, challenges, and workshops like SemEval-2022 (Task 3), QASR-TTS-v1.0 (ASRU2023), SLT2023 (Local Chair), summer workshop JSALT2022 (as a senior mentor) along with serving in the program-committee of top-tier conferences and special interest groups (SIGs).

Sabri Boughorbel is a Scientist at QCRI, HBKU. He received his PhD in Machine Learning from the university of Paris Sud. He has an extensive experience in Machine Learning for industrial and academic research. He authored more than 70 peer-reviewed papers and 7 patents. He was awarded several grants in the intersection of machine learning and health. His current research is on leveraging open-sourced LLMs for low-resource languages and developing multi-modal language models. He serves as PC member of top-tier machine learning conferences. In 2023, he co-organized a workshop on AI for Medicine.

Maram Hasanain is a PostDoctoral researcher at QCRI, HBKU. She received her PhD in Computer Science from Qatar University. Her current research interests are Arabic NLP, applied machine learning, and LLMs. Maram co-authored over 25 peer-reviewed publications in top-tier conferences and journals. She has been a co-organizer in the CheckThat! lab at CLEF 2019-2021, 2023 and 2024. She was also a co-organizer of the BroDyn'18 workshop on analysis of broad dynamic topics over social media co-located with ECIR'18.

7 Ethics Statement

Our tutorial is based on our own work in the area, related studies and public sources. Credit will be given wherever needed. Any biases are unintended.

Acknowledgments

The contributions of M. Hasanain were funded by the NPRP grant 14C-0916-210015, which is provided by the Qatar National Research Fund (a member of Qatar Foundation).

References

Ahmed Abdelali, Hamdy Mubarak, Shammur Absar Chowdhury, Maram Hasanain, Basel Mousi, Sabri Boughorbel, Yassine El Kheir, Daniel Izham, Fahim Dalvi, Majd Hawasly, et al. 2023. Benchmarking arabic ai with large language models. *arXiv preprint arXiv:2305.14982*.

Kabir Ahuja, Harshita Diddee, Rishav Hada, Millicent Ochieng, Krithika Ramesh, Prachi Jain, Akshay Nambi, Tanuja Ganu, Sameer Segal, Mohamed Ahmed, Kalika Bali, and Sunayana Sitaram. 2023. MEGA: Multilingual evaluation of generative AI.

In *Proceedings of the 2023 Conference on Empirical Methods in Natural Language Processing*, pages 4232–4267, Singapore. Association for Computational Linguistics.

Yejin Bang, Samuel Cahyawijaya, Nayeon Lee, Wenliang Dai, Dan Su, Bryan Wilie, Holy Lovenia, Ziwei Ji, Tiezheng Yu, Willy Chung, et al. 2023. A multitask, multilingual, multimodal evaluation of ChatGPT on reasoning, hallucination, and interactivity. *arXiv preprint arXiv:2302.04023*.

Tom B. Brown, Benjamin Mann, Nick Ryder, Melanie Subbiah, Jared Kaplan, Prafulla Dhariwal, Arvind Neelakantan, Pranav Shyam, Girish Sastry, Amanda Askell, Sandhini Agarwal, Ariel Herbert-Voss, Gretchen Krueger, Tom Henighan, Rewon Child, Aditya Ramesh, Daniel M. Ziegler, Jeffrey Wu, Clemens Winter, Christopher Hesse, Mark Chen, Eric Sigler, Mateusz Litwin, Scott Gray, Benjamin Chess, Jack Clark, Christopher Berner, Sam McCandlish, Alec Radford, Ilya Sutskever, and Dario Amodei. 2020. Language models are few-shot learners. *Advances in Neural Information Processing Systems*.

Sébastien Bubeck, Varun Chandrasekaran, Ronen Eldan, Johannes Gehrke, Eric Horvitz, Ece Kamar, Peter Lee, Yin Tat Lee, Yuanzhi Li, Scott Lundberg, Harsha Nori, Hamid Palangi, Marco Tulio Ribeiro, and Yi Zhang. 2023. Sparks of artificial general intelligence: Early experiments with GPT-4. Technical report, Microsoft Research.

Jaime Carbonell and Jade Goldstein. 1998. The use of mmr, diversity-based reranking for reordering documents and producing summaries. In *Proceedings of the 21st annual international ACM SIGIR conference on Research and development in information retrieval*, pages 335–336.

Wei-Lin Chiang, Zhuohan Li, Zi Lin, Ying Sheng, Zhanghao Wu, Hao Zhang, Lianmin Zheng, Siyuan Zhuang, Yonghao Zhuang, Joseph E Gonzalez, et al. 2023. Vicuna: An open-source chatbot impressing gpt-4 with 90%* chatgpt quality. *See https://vicuna. lmsys. org (accessed 14 April 2023)*.

Fahim Dalvi, Maram Hasanain, Sabri Boughorbel, Basel Mousi, Samir Abdaljalil, Nizi Nazar, Ahmed Abdelali, Shammur Absar Chowdhury, Hamdy Mubarak, Ahmed Ali, Majd Hawasly, Nadir Durrani, and Firoj Alam. 2023. LLMeBench: a flexible framework for accelerating LLMs benchmarking. *arXiv 2308.04945*.

Jacob Devlin, Ming-Wei Chang, Kenton Lee, and Kristina Toutanova. 2019. BERT: Pre-training of deep bidirectional transformers for language understanding. In *Proceedings of the 2019 Conference of the North American Chapter of the Association for Computational Linguistics: Human Language Technologies*, pages 4171–4186.

Qingxiu Dong, Lei Li, Damai Dai, Ce Zheng, Zhiyong Wu, Baobao Chang, Xu Sun, Jingjing Xu, and Zhifang Sui. 2022. A survey for in-context learning. *arXiv preprint arXiv:2301.00234*.

Leo Gao, Jonathan Tow, Baber Abbasi, Stella Biderman, Sid Black, Anthony DiPofi, Charles Foster, Laurence Golding, Jeffrey Hsu, Alain Le Noac'h, Haonan Li, Kyle McDonell, Niklas Muennighoff, Chris Ociepa, Jason Phang, Laria Reynolds, Hailey Schoelkopf, Aviya Skowron, Lintang Sutawika, Eric Tang, Anish Thite, Ben Wang, Kevin Wang, and Andy Zou. 2023. A framework for few-shot language model evaluation. *Zenodo*.

Jindong Gu, Zhen Han, Shuo Chen, Ahmad Beirami, Bailan He, Gengyuan Zhang, Ruotong Liao, Yao Qin, Volker Tresp, and Philip Torr. 2023. A systematic survey of prompt engineering on vision-language foundation models. *arXiv preprint arXiv:2307.12980*.

Md. Arid Hasan, Shudipta Das, Afiyat Anjum, Firoj Alam, Anika Anjum, Avijit Sarker, and Sheak Rashed Haider Noori. 2023. Zero- and few-shot prompting with llms: A comparative study with fine-tuned models for bangla sentiment analysis. *arXiv preprint arXiv:2308.10783*.

Amr Hendy, Mohamed Abdelrehim, Amr Sharaf, Vikas Raunak, Mohamed Gabr, Hitokazu Matsushita, Young Jin Kim, Mohamed Afify, and Hany Hassan Awadalla. 2023. How good are GPT models at machine translation? a comprehensive evaluation. *arXiv preprint arXiv:2302.09210*.

Md Tawkat Islam Khondaker, Abdul Waheed, El Moatez Billah Nagoudi, and Muhammad Abdul-Mageed. 2023. Gptaraeval: A comprehensive evaluation of chatgpt on arabic nlp. *arXiv preprint arXiv:2305.14976*.

Taku Kudo and John Richardson. 2018. Sentencepiece: A simple and language independent subword tokenizer and detokenizer for neural text processing. In *Proceedings of the 2018 Conference on Empirical Methods in Natural Language Processing: System Demonstrations*, pages 66–71.

Viet Dac Lai, Nghia Trung Ngo, Amir Pouran Ben Veyseh, Hieu Man, Franck Dernoncourt, Trung Bui, and Thien Huu Nguyen. 2023. ChatGPT beyond english: Towards a comprehensive evaluation of large language models in multilingual learning. *arXiv preprint arXiv:2304.05613*.

Mike Lewis, Yinhan Liu, Naman Goyal, Marjan Ghazvininejad, Abdelrahman Mohamed, Omer Levy, Veselin Stoyanov, and Luke Zettlemoyer. 2020. BART: Denoising sequence-to-sequence pre-training for natural language generation, translation, and comprehension. In *Proceedings of the 58th Annual Meeting of the Association for Computational Linguistics*, pages 7871–7880.

Junnan Li, Dongxu Li, Silvio Savarese, and Steven Hoi. 2023. Blip-2: Bootstrapping language-image pre-training with frozen image encoders and large language models. *arXiv preprint arXiv:2301.12597*.

Percy Liang, Rishi Bommasani, Tony Lee, Dimitris Tsipras, Dilara Soylu, Michihiro Yasunaga, Yian Zhang, Deepak Narayanan, Yuhuai Wu, Ananya Kumar, et al. 2022. Holistic evaluation of language models. *arXiv preprint arXiv:2211.09110*.

Haotian Liu, Chunyuan Li, Qingyang Wu, and Yong Jae Lee. 2023a. Visual instruction tuning. *arXiv:2304.08485*.

Pengfei Liu, Weizhe Yuan, Jinlan Fu, Zhengbao Jiang, Hiroaki Hayashi, and Graham Neubig. 2023b. Pre-train, prompt, and predict: A systematic survey of prompting methods in natural language processing. *ACM Computing Surveys*, 55(9):1–35.

Yinhan Liu, Myle Ott, Naman Goyal, Jingfei Du, Mandar Joshi, Danqi Chen, Omer Levy, Mike Lewis, Luke Zettlemoyer, and Veselin Stoyanov. 2019. RoBERTa: A robustly optimized bert pretraining approach. *arXiv preprint arXiv:1907.11692*.

Sabrina J Mielke, Zaid Alyafeai, Elizabeth Salesky, Colin Raffel, Manan Dey, Matthias Gallé, Arun Raja, Chenglei Si, Wilson Y Lee, Benoît Sagot, et al. 2021. Between words and characters: A brief history of open-vocabulary modeling and tokenization in nlp. *arXiv preprint arXiv:2112.10508*.

Seungwhan Moon, Andrea Madotto, Zhaojiang Lin, Tushar Nagarajan, Matt Smith, Shashank Jain, Chun-Fu Yeh, Prakash Murugesan, Peyman Heidari, Yue Liu, et al. 2023. Anymal: An efficient and scalable any-modality augmented language model. *arXiv preprint arXiv:2309.16058*.

OpenAI. 2023a. Gpt-4 technical report.

OpenAI. 2023b. Gpt-4v(ision) system card. *OpenAI*.

Alec Radford, Jong Wook Kim, Tao Xu, Greg Brockman, Christine McLeavey, and Ilya Sutskever. 2022. Robust speech recognition via large-scale weak supervision. *arXiv preprint arXiv:2212.04356*.

Alec Radford, Jeffrey Wu, Rewon Child, David Luan, Dario Amodei, Ilya Sutskever, et al. 2019. Language models are unsupervised multitask learners. *OpenAI blog*, 1(8):9.

Laria Reynolds and Kyle McDonell. 2021. Prompt programming for large language models: Beyond the few-shot paradigm. In *Extended Abstracts of the 2021 CHI Conference on Human Factors in Computing Systems*, pages 1–7.

Teven Le Scao, Angela Fan, Christopher Akiki, Ellie Pavlick, Suzana Ilić, Daniel Hesslow, Roman Castagné, Alexandra Sasha Luccioni, François Yvon, Matthias Gallé, et al. 2022. Bloom: A 176b-parameter open-access multilingual language model. *arXiv preprint arXiv:2211.05100*.

Rico Sennrich, Barry Haddow, and Alexandra Birch. 2016. Neural machine translation of rare words with subword units. In *Proceedings of the 54th Annual Meeting of the Association for Computational Linguistics (Volume 1: Long Papers)*, pages 1715–1725.

Aarohi Srivastava, Abhinav Rastogi, Abhishek Rao, Abu Awal Md Shoeb, Abubakar Abid, Adam Fisch, Adam R Brown, Adam Santoro, Aditya Gupta, Adrià Garriga-Alonso, et al. 2022. Beyond the imitation game: Quantifying and extrapolating the capabilities of language models. *arXiv preprint arXiv:2206.04615*.

Gemini Team, Rohan Anil, Sebastian Borgeaud, Yonghui Wu, Jean-Baptiste Alayrac, Jiahui Yu, Radu Soricut, Johan Schalkwyk, Andrew M Dai, Anja Hauth, et al. 2023. Gemini: a family of highly capable multimodal models. *arXiv preprint arXiv:2312.11805*.

Hugo Touvron, Thibaut Lavril, Gautier Izacard, Xavier Martinet, Marie-Anne Lachaux, Timothée Lacroix, Baptiste Rozière, Naman Goyal, Eric Hambro, Faisal Azhar, et al. 2023. LLaMA: Open and efficient foundation language models. *arXiv preprint arXiv:2302.13971*.

Ashish Vaswani, Noam Shazeer, Niki Parmar, Jakob Uszkoreit, Llion Jones, Aidan N Gomez, Łukasz Kaiser, and Illia Polosukhin. 2017. Attention is all you need. *Advances in neural information processing systems*, 30.

Jason Wei, Maarten Bosma, Vincent Y Zhao, Kelvin Guu, Adams Wei Yu, Brian Lester, Nan Du, Andrew M Dai, and Quoc V Le. 2021. Finetuned language models are zero-shot learners. *arXiv preprint arXiv:2109.01652*.

Yonghui Wu, Mike Schuster, Zhifeng Chen, Quoc V Le, Mohammad Norouzi, Wolfgang Macherey, Maxim Krikun, Yuan Cao, Qin Gao, Klaus Macherey, et al. 2016. Google's neural machine translation system: Bridging the gap between human and machine translation. *arXiv preprint arXiv:1609.08144*.

Zhenyu Wu, Yaoxiang Wang, Jiacheng Ye, Zhiyong Wu, Jiangtao Feng, Jingjing Xu, and Yu Qiao. 2023. OpenICL: An open-source framework for in-context learning. In *Proceedings of the 61st Annual Meeting of the Association for Computational Linguistics (Volume 3: System Demonstrations)*, pages 489–498.

Linting Xue, Noah Constant, Adam Roberts, Mihir Kale, Rami Al-Rfou, Aditya Siddhant, Aditya Barua, and Colin Raffel. 2020. mt5: A massively multilingual pre-trained text-to-text transformer. *arXiv preprint arXiv:2010.11934*.

Shu-wen Yang, Po-Han Chi, Yung-Sung Chuang, Cheng-I Jeff Lai, Kushal Lakhotia, Yist Y Lin, Andy T Liu, Jiatong Shi, Xuankai Chang, Guan-Ting Lin, et al. 2021. Superb: Speech processing universal performance benchmark. *arXiv preprint arXiv:2105.01051*.

Yu Zhang, Wei Han, James Qin, Yongqiang Wang, Ankur Bapna, Zhehuai Chen, Nanxin Chen, Bo Li, Vera Axelrod, Gary Wang, Zhong Meng, Ke Hu, Andrew Rosenberg, Rohit Prabhavalkar, Daniel S. Park, Parisa Haghani, Jason Riesa, Ginger Perng, Hagen Soltau, Trevor Strohman, Bhuvana Ramabhadran, Tara Sainath, Pedro Moreno, Chung-Cheng Chiu, Johan Schalkwyk, Françoise Beaufays, and Yonghui Wu. 2023. Google usm: Scaling automatic speech recognition beyond 100 languages. *arXiv preprint arXiv:2303.01037*.

Zhuosheng Zhang, Aston Zhang, Mu Li, and Alex Smola. 2022. Automatic chain of thought prompting in large language models. *arXiv preprint arXiv:2210.03493*.

Wayne Xin Zhao, Kun Zhou, Junyi Li, Tianyi Tang, Xiaolei Wang, Yupeng Hou, Yingqian Min, Beichen Zhang, Junjie Zhang, Zican Dong, et al. 2023. A survey of large language models. *arXiv preprint arXiv:2303.18223*.

Deyao Zhu, Jun Chen, Xiaoqian Shen, Xiang Li, and Mohamed Elhoseiny. 2023a. MiniGPT-4: Enhancing vision-language understanding with advanced large language models. *arXiv preprint arXiv:2304.10592*.

Kaijie Zhu, Jindong Wang, Jiaheng Zhou, Zichen Wang, Hao Chen, Yidong Wang, Linyi Yang, Wei Ye, Neil Zhenqiang Gong, Yue Zhang, et al. 2023b. PromptBench: Towards evaluating the robustness of large language models on adversarial prompts. *arXiv preprint arXiv:2306.04528*.

Author Index